KNOWING CHILDREN:
EXPERIMENTS IN CONVERSATION AND COGNITION

Michael Siegal

University of Queensland, Australia

LEA LAWRENCE ERLBAUM ASSOCIATES, PUBLISHERS LEA
Hove and London (UK)   Hillsdale (USA)

Lawrence Erlbaum Associates Ltd., Publishers
27 Palmeira Mansions
Church Road
Hove
East Sussex, BN3 2FA
U.K.

British Library Cataloguing in Publication Data
Siegal, Michael
    Knowing children: experiments in conversation and
        cognition
    (Essays in developmental psychology)
    1. Children. Cognitive development related to
        acquisition of language skills
    I. Title
    155.413
    ISBN 0-86377-158-0 (HBK)
    ISBN 0-86377-159-9 (PBK)
    ISSN 0959-3977 (Essays in Developmental Psychology)

Typeset by The Laverham Press, Salisbury
Printed and bound by BPCC Wheatons, Exeter

KNOWING CHILDREN

Contents

Preface

Anyone who knows children realises that they have an understanding which often is not reflected in what they say and do. A concerned adult tries to draw out their knowledge patiently. However, this may not be easy. It is common to attribute children's difficulties in answering questions on the many experimental tasks that have traditionally been used to determine their understanding to a basic limitation in their intellectual or cognitive development.

In this essay, I propose that children's apparently poor performance can frequently be explained in terms of a clash between the conversational worlds of adults and children. Young children may not share the assumption that the purpose of an experiment is the scientific one of establishing their understanding of concepts. They may inadvertently perceive an adult's well-meaning questions to be ambiguous, irrelevant, insincere, or uninformative. In addition, an experimenter may unjustifiably assume that children will share the use of certain words that are prerequisites for understanding questions. Unlike adults are who are experienced in conversation and can recognise the implications that flow from different forms of questioning, young children are liable to misinterpret an experimenter's purpose or use of language. They may respond incorrectly, not because they do not know the answer, but because the conversational worlds of adults and children diverge.

Yet if given the opportunity, young children often astutely attribute incorrect answers to adult questions to features of the conversational environment. Once this environment is given support, they are more likely to disclose what they know. I do not propose that they have a full-blown understanding, only an *implicit* one that constrains their learning and that may be used to enhance their knowledge.

The point that adult forms of communication may obscure an authentic understanding is hardly new (Donaldson, 1978; Light, Buckingham, & Robins, 1979) and has been noted by Vygotsky (1962) and in related accounts of early development (e.g., Rogoff & Wertsch, 1984). All the same, to give due regard to communication difficulties requires systematic tests of how children interpret conversation. There are now experiments where efforts have been made to investigate how children understand the nature and purpose of adults' questions. The results indicate that children have a greater knowledge than has been commonly estimated (e.g., Piaget, 1970; Sugarman, 1987).

The disparity between the conversational worlds of adults and children and the consequences for children's responses in experiments are documented in the following chapters. The implications for instruction in subjects such as mathematics and science are significant.

Acknowledgements

The work reported here spans two sabbatical leaves: at McGill University in the fall of 1986 and the University of California, Los Angeles, in early 1990. The ideas were developed further in discussions at the University of Pennsylvania in January 1988, the University of Pittsburgh in February 1989, and the University of Otago, New Zealand, in September 1989. I am very grateful to those in Australia and overseas who have given suggestions and advice, and to my students and colleagues: Mary Barclay, Jan Cowen, Simon Dinwiddy, Yoshi Kashima, Robyn Nugent, Jenny Sanderson, David Share, and Lorraine Waters. The shortcomings are of course mine alone. Some of the research described in this article was supported by grants from the Australian Research Council and the National Health and Medical Research Council.

Tables 3.1 and 3.2 originally appeared in *Child Development* and are reproduced by permission of the Society for Research in Child Development. Figures 1.1 and Table 3.3 originally appeared in *Developmental Psychology* and are reproduced by permission of the authors (copyright by the American Psychological Association). Figure 2.1 is adapted from the *Journal of Experimental Child Psychology* (published by Academic Press, Inc.). Figure 3.1 is reproduced by permission of the author and Harvard University Press. Figure 4.1 from *The Child's Conception of Space* by Jean Piaget and Barbel Inhelder is reproduced by permission of Routledge & Kegan Paul. Part of Chapter 4 has been adapted from an article that appeared in *Cognition*, *31*, (1989) 277–280, co-authored by Jennifer A. Sanderson.

This book is dedicated to the memory of my father.

M.S.
August, 1990

ix

1 What Children Know Before Talking

The answer to the question, "To what extent can young children under-stand abstract concepts?" is central to research on child development. One view, expressed forcefully by the great Swiss psychologist, Jean Piaget (1970), is that young children's knowledge of the world is largely limited to perceptual appearances and that they are incapable of insight into the minds of others. At their own pace, the vast majority will eventually move out of a stage of development marked by severe limitations on the ability to understand concepts.

Over a period of more than 40 years, Piaget came up with a wide variety of evidence from observations and interviews. On this basis, he argued that preschool children were not capable of logical thinking and that their stage of development could be best described as "preoperational". Piaget and his followers maintained that education should have the modest goal of matching the child's stage level. These ideas have had a major impact on educational programmes. Many people have either accepted the view that young children are not ready for instruction—especially in subjects like mathematics and science—or have claimed that programmes should be designed basically to extend children's awareness of the world beyond that of thinking about perceptual appearances.

My aim in this essay is to demonstrate that young children actually know a good deal about abstract concepts, for example, of causality, and the identity of persons and objects. The apparent contradiction in the evidence is resolved by a very different explanation that focuses on language. My idea is that children are both sophisticated and limited users of the rules of conversation that promote effective communication: sophisticated when it comes to the use of conversational rules in everyday, natural talk; limited in specialised settings which require knowledge of the purpose intended by speakers who have set aside the rules that characterise the conventional use of language. Such situations may often involve children in experiments where they inadvertently perceive adults' well-meaning questions as redundant, insincere, irrelevant, uninformative, or ambiguous.

There are now experiments where efforts have been made to follow conversational rules in order to ensure that children understand the nature and purpose of adults' questions. The results demonstrate that children do have a substantially greater knowledge of abstract concepts than Piaget estimated, and demand a significant shift in educational implications. For example, if preschoolers are able to understand how effects can be caused by factors that are not visible, they should know that food with an apparently fresh appearance may, in reality, be contaminated. This would warrant placing a greater emphasis on early preventive health education. Similarly, if young children are able to understand that there are fractions which fill the gaps between whole numbers, a more intensive instruction in the use of symbolic principles of mathematics would be in order.

MODELS OF DEVELOPMENT AND DEVELOPMENTAL COGNITIVE SCIENCE

Since the young have little experience in communication, those such as Piaget who at times claim that they are limited in the ability to understand concepts must ensure that failure can be attributed to a "deep" lack of ability rather than to some misreading of the experimenter's intent in asking questions. Moreover, children can have a grasp of a concept and properly interpret the experimenter's intent, yet they may still fail owing to memory difficulties, a lack of familiarity with words or linguistic forms, or a lack of sophisticated motor behaviour. To provide a more accurate characterisation, a model of development is required that proposes a "conceptual competence" which is implicit within the mind of the child.

This type of model building goes beyond traditional disciplinary boundaries and has been increasingly studied in the field of cognitive science, an amalgam of many disciplines including anthropology, computer science, linguistics, neuroscience, philosophy, and psychology. Linguistics in particular would dictate that any comprehensive study of children's abilities must take into account their interpretation of conversational rules to ensure that their lack of success on tasks that involve knowledge of abstract concepts cannot be attributed to infringements of these rules.

The tasks designed to test children's understanding almost invariably require a degree of language comprehension. In this respect, adult experimenters may seek to determine that children have a particular concept through direct questioning or through prolonged questioning on numerous similar tasks. However, ordinarily we do not repeat requests when an answer has already been given. This is a convention or rule of conversation that promotes communication through non-redundant messages. A gap may emerge between the intent of the experimenter (which is to make a certain judgement about what children know) and children's experience with methods of repeated or other forms of unconventional questioning. In such cases, they may misinterpret these requests as conveying the necessity to respond inconsistently or in an "appropriate" way to satisfy what they perceive as expected. In addition, experimenters may use words such as "number" or "same" which can have different meanings for children than for adults. Because children's responses on many tasks critically hinge on the interpretation of the use of language, any failures cannot be easily attributed to a deep lack of conceptual ability. A lack of performance may instead be due to children's "interpretative theory" of the purpose and meanings of linguistic forms used in the experiment.

No doubt a large part of development can be viewed in terms of children's understanding of language and communication. With increasing experience, an implicit conceptual ability may be expressed more explicitly in words regardless of whether experimenters follow conversational rules. In my opinion, part of what distinguishes developmental psychology from research with adults in perception, cognition, and social psychology is a methodology specifically directed towards examining children's understanding of abstract concepts as distinct from their comprehension of language. To demonstrate this understanding requires novel methodologies and clever experimentation.

The matter is further complicated in efforts to establish that the rudiments of abstract concepts may be within the grasp of preverbal infants. Not only do infants lack speech (indeed, the word "infant" itself is derived from the Latin *infans*, or the unspeaking one) but, given their restricted motor development, we cannot even rely on their searching or crawling to shed light on their understanding. Even so, the use in testing situations of innovative methods of communicating with infants has increasingly revealed their implicit knowledge. As a guiding model, child development is better characterised by development towards the conscious accessibility of implicit knowledge rather than a simple lack of conceptual ability or coherence.

In the 19th century, two prominent theorists found a place for this type of developmental model. Yet in each case, it was not until recently that the more important of their two major propositions has been accorded recognition. First, the German physicist and physiologist, Hermann von Helmholtz (see Warren & Warren, 1968) advocated the empiricist position that, for the most part, children's perception of the world is not innate but is determined by an unconscious association of ideas in memory that depends on past experience. This is the most enduring legacy of Helmholtz's writings. It has predominated at the expense of his second proposition that the mechanism for making inferences about these ideas is itself innate. According to Helmholtz, "the law of causation, by virtue of which we infer the cause from the effect, has to be considered also as being a law of our thinking which is prior to all experience. Generally, we can get no experience from natural objects unless the law of causation is already active in us. Therefore, it cannot be deduced first from experiences which we have had with natural objects" (Warren & Warren, 1968, p. 201). On this basis, it has been recognised that young children may be equipped with the ability to make "perceptual" inferences which can be developed through instruction (Bryant, 1974).

The other 19th century developmental theorist is Charles Darwin (1859). His contribution to experimental psychology cannot be underrated and consists of two major legacies. The first was the emphasis on similarities in the evolution and structure of animal and human behaviour. Accordingly, certain principles of animal psychology have been seen to apply as well to humans (Passingham, 1982). Darwin's second proposition concerned the diversity of organisms and their adaptive fit with the environment, and has only recently been acknowledged as meriting the more fundamental recognition (Rozin & Schull, 1988). On this basis, biological species may be viewed as constrained to learn adaptive behaviours. In particular, although the idea has yet to be fully exploited, human children may be constrained to learn behaviour such as parenting, predator avoidance, sheltering, and the procurement of nutrients through developing the accessibility of their innate or early abilities (Rozin, 1976; Rozin & Schull, 1988).

The findings of modern research on preschoolers and children in the early primary school years are foreshadowed in the writings of Helmholtz and Darwin. However, the astonishing performance of infants in experiments provides some of the most graphic illustrations of early implicit knowledge. This research sets the stage to examine young children's understanding of abstract concepts.

OBJECT PERMANENCE

One of Piaget's (1954) major claims was that infants are at a "sensorimotor" stage in development. By way of foreshadowing the limitations of preoperational young children, he maintained that infants do not understand objects as permanent entities which continue to exist while out of sight. For Piaget, this basic "object concept" is not achieved until they can reach out to uncover hidden objects. Yet even at 9 months, infants do not search for an object seen hidden in a new location if they have been used to finding an object in a familiar one. The inability to recover an object in a new place suggests that infants lack object permanence.

One interpretation of this result is that they expect that a formerly successful response will produce the object regardless of where it has been hidden. In fact, however, a searching response does not necessarily reflect sophistication on the part of infants. Searching may be based, first, on their knowledge of the function of containment (Freeman, Lloyd, & Sinha, 1980) or, second, on their knowledge that there are many similar objects and these are often duplicated (Bremner & Knowles, 1984). A third, straightforward alternative is that infants possess object permanence but lack the ability to perform co-ordinated actions by shifting the focus of their attention to a new location. If so, their searching behaviour may not be a fully adequate measure of their understanding.

A recent ingenious study carried out by Renée Baillargeon and her co-workers (Baillargeon, Spelke, & Wasserman, 1985) has shown that infants as young as five months of age understand that objects exist when hidden. Babies were "habituated" to a screen that moved back and forth through a 180-degree arc in the manner of a drawbridge until they were used to viewing the action of the screen and became clearly inattentive. Then they were shown a box centred behind the screen, and viewed two types of events: one that was possible and one that was not. In the possible event, the screen stopped when the box was hidden. In the impossible event, the screen went right through the space that the box had occupied. The surprised and attentive reaction of the infants to the impossible event was taken to illustrate their knowledge that objects continue to exist when concealed. This result is compatible with a proposal made by Kellman, Spelke, and Short (1986): infants anticipate that the movements of objects are constrained by rigid structures and expect that the unity and nature of objects depends on coherent movement.

In later experiments, Baillargeon and Graber (1988) examined 8-month-olds' memory for the location of objects. The infants first viewed an object (an inverted white styrofoam cup decorated with stars, dots, and pushpins) standing on one of two placemats. A screen was then pushed in front of each placemat shielding the object from sight. After a 15-second interval, a hand wearing a silver glove and a bracelet of jingle bells reached behind one of the screens and emerged with the object. The infants were tested under two conditions. In the "possible event" condition, the object was retrieved from behind a screen that shielded the location where it had been seen hidden. In the "impossible event" condition, the object was retrieved from behind a screen that shielded a different location (see Fig. 1.1). Infants looked at the object longer in the impossible event condition.

Possible Event   **Impossible Event**

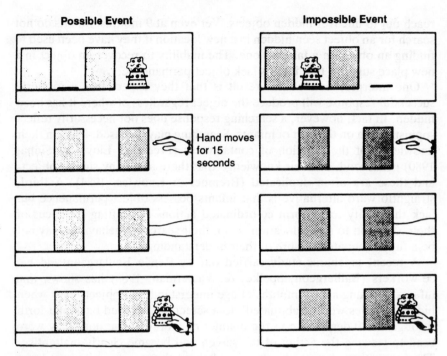

FIG. 1.1   An illustration of the test events shown to 8-month-old infants (from Baillargeon & Graber, 1988).

Apparently, they were surprised to see that it had been retrieved from behind the screen which did not shield the original hiding place. Although many infants may not accurately search for an object, they can still remember where it was before it had been concealed. Their responses undermine Piaget's position on object permanence—that infants' lack of success on searching tasks is due to a conceptual limitation.

Baillargeon's experiments have shown how habituation techniques can be used as a method to communicate with infants. In general, the younger the child, the more likely an habitual or repeated presentation of the task will create disinterest. A long delay between concealing an object and the opportunity for retrieval may induce infants to fall back on an earlier hiding place where the object has been found on previous occasions (Diamond, 1985). A new and unexpected situation may recapture infants' attention and permit a more genuine appraisal of their abilities.

The lack of object permanence in Piaget's studies can also in part be attributed to an unfamiliar situation in which infants can respond by focusing their attention on the location of the mother. Presson and Ihrig (1982) placed 30 9-month-olds in a spatial location procedure in which the task was to respond to pictures of animals and people. The infants used the mother as a landmark to guide their responses. When the mother's position was stable and did not provide a cue to repeat a previous response, they were able to find the correct location of the pictures.

IMITATION OF FACIAL EXPRESSIONS

An understanding of object relations may emerge from a capacity in newborns to learn through imitation. In a series of experiments reported in 1977, Meltzoff and Moore tested the proposition that infants between 12- and 21-days-of-age can imitate both facial and manual gestures. Six infants in a first experiment were shown the non-reactive, passive face of an experimenter for a 90-second period. Then 4 gestures were each repeated 4 times in a random order during a 15-second stimulus-presentation period immediately followed by a 20-second response period in which the experimenter resumed a passive face. The infants were observed to imitate the gestures of the experimenter: finger movements, opening of the mouth, and protrusion of the tongue and lips.

A second study was designed to rule out the possibility that interaction between the experimenter and infant might have resulted in a form of "pseudo-imitation": that is, the infants' own random gestures might have altered those of the experimenter until their behaviour coincided with behaviour resembling imitation. Infants were shown the experimenter's mouth opening and tongue protrusion gestures for 15 seconds while sucking attentively on a pacifier. They imitated the gestures when the pacifier was removed. In a similar manner, Tiffany Field and her colleagues (Field, Woodson, Greenberg, & Cohen, 1982) found that newborns imitated an experimenter's happy, sad, and angry expressions.

Not all the data clearly indicates imitation in the newborn (see Lewis & Sullivan, 1985; McKenzie & Over, 1983). Yet there is now widespread agreement that babies can imitate by 6 months-of-age, long before Piaget's estimate of between 8 months to a year. In fact, it can be speculated that a capacity for representation which may facilitate infants' responses is present at birth. In a study of hand–mouth co-ordination, Butterworth and Hopkins (1988) filmed the spontaneous motor activity of 15 newborns. They found that the mouth was open "in anticipation" of the arrival of the hand and that this movement was not related to guidance by the eye.

IDENTIFICATION OF VOICES AND SOUNDS

If infants can imitate at an early age, when might they be able to identify voices and sounds? To address this question, DeCasper and Fifer (1980) asked the mothers of 10 infants (younger than 3-days-of-age) to read Dr. Suess's book, *To Think That I Saw It On Mulberry Street*. Their voices were tape-recorded. By sucking on a nipple in long and short patterns of bursts, the infants could control whether they would hear the story read by their own mother or another mother. Infants showed a significant preference for their own mother. Since postnatal mother–infant verbal interaction did not relate to their responses, DeCasper and Fifer interpreted the data to indicate that infants' preference for the mother's voice develops in utero.

Using the sucking technique, it has also been shown that somewhat older infants can distinguish between different sounds in a categorical fashion much as adults do. Eimas and Miller (1980) presented 2- to 4-month-olds with synthetic speech patterns consisting of combinations of the stop consonant [b] and the semivowel [w]. An increase in the number of high amplitude sucking responses per minute was taken as a measure of their ability to discriminate between stop consonants and the semivowels. The infants' rate of sucking increased with the transition in the acoustic information. In addition, as in adults, the ability to discriminate sounds was influenced by the duration of the transition and the length of the syllables. More recently, using a modified version of the high amplitude sucking technique, newborns have shown some ability to represent differences in a set of syllables (Bertoncini et al., 1988).

Newborns also have some ability to make connections between vision and sound. Perhaps the most interesting demonstration remains the series of experiments conducted by Mendleson and Haith (1976). For example, babies aged 1 to 4 days were placed on their backs facing up to a television camera. They then heard 10 auditory stimuli such as the following:

Hello Baby. It's really nice to see you here today. Believe it or not, you're on television right now. If the folks back home could only see you, wouldn't they be surprised? I hope that you'll keep your eyes open nice and wide and please, Baby, try not to move your head around too much. That's the only way we'll get a good videotape of you. If you co-operate really well you'll have the satisfaction of knowing that you've helped Science find truth and understanding. And remember, Baby, "Truth is beauty, beauty truth." Thank you for trying so hard, Baby. Have a nice day.

In response to this message, infants turned their heads and looked towards the location of the sound. They demonstrated a capacity for using sound to guide their visual exploration.

By the age of 4 months, there is an expectation that sounds correspond to sights. In the first of 4 experiments, Spelke (1981) presented 3- to 4-month-olds with pairs of films. During an initial familiarisation procedure, they watched kangaroos and donkeys bouncing to a soundtrack synchronised to either a gong or a thumping sound. Then, in a test period, the sounds were placed out of synchrony. The infants looked first at the animal that had previously bounced in synchrony. Later experiments confirmed that the ability to match sound with sight can be transferred to new information and is not specific to the spatial position of visual stimuli.

MATCHING TOUCH WITH VISION

The ability of infants to use touch as a basis for visual recognition was shown in a series of experiments by Bryant, Jones, Claxton, and Perkins (1972). In a first experiment, 60 infants between 6- and 11-months-of-age were given a task consisting of 3 phases. The infants were initially shown two objects that were out of reach on a table: one object was a complete shape (e.g., a cube) and the other was incomplete (e.g., a cube with a piece missing). In the second phase, they were given one of the objects to hold, unseen, containing a bleeper activated by a mercury switch when tilted. In the third test phase, the pairs were presented again and the number reading for the previously held object was observed. In this experiment and a subsequent one, infants often reached for the object that they had felt in their hands. A significant number made the match from touch to vision.

Meltzoff and Borton (1979) demonstrated that infants aged from 26 to 33 days could also match across modalities. In a first experiment, 32 infants were given a small hard rubber pacifier to place in their mouths for 90 seconds. Then the stimulus was removed. The babies' visual preferences were tested by presenting them with two shapes made from dense styrofoam and painted orange. One shape matched that of the small hard rubber pacifier and the other was different. During a 20-second test, infants preferred to look at the object that they had previously explored orally. The results were replicated in a second experiment using a different group of infants and a different experimenter. Similarly, in more recent work, Gibson and Walker (1984) gave 12-month-olds a hard or elastic, spongy substance to explore orally for 60 seconds. The infants preferred to look more at a visual depiction of the familiar substance that at the alternative choice.

PERCEPTION OF NUMBER AND CAUSAL RELATIONS

The ability to detect changes in small numbers and to identify correspondences between seeing numbers and hearing a sequence of sounds has also been demonstrated in a recent series of experiments. Starkey and Cooper (1980) gave infants with a mean age of 22 weeks (range, 16 to 30 weeks) arrays containing 2, 3, 4, and 6 dots. Once the infants habituated to these arrays, they were given other ones containing a different number of dots: the 2-dot array was replaced by 3 dots, the 3-dot by 2 dots, the 4-dot by 6 dots, and the 6-dot by 4 dots. In the case of the 2- and 3-dot arrays, the infants dishabituated and looked significantly longer at the new stimuli. Similar results have been reported based on a sample of newborns with a mean age of 53 hours and a range of 21 to 144 hours (Antell & Keating, 1983).

Starkey, Spelke, and Gelman (1983) have further established that infants prefer to look at arrays of objects which correspond in number to sound sequences. In their experiments, 7-month-olds viewed pairs of slides of 2 or 3 heterogeneous objects (e.g., a memo pad and comb vs. a bell pepper, animal horn, and scissors). Two or three beats of a drum accompanied each slide presentation. The infants attended to the two-object array longer when it was accompanied by two drumbeats, and the three-object array when it was accompanied by three drumbeats. These findings are compatible with the notion that knowledge of arithmetic develops from an early sensitivity to correspondence between number.

Other work by Leslie and Keeble (1987) has suggested that 6-month-old infants may already have the capacity to perceive cause-and-effect relations. In two experiments, infants were shown films of apparently causal events and non-causal events. In the film of the causal event, a "direct launching" was depicted: a bright red brick moved a bright green brick on impact. In the film of the non-causal event, the green brick moved as a delayed action. About a minute after the infants had habituated to the sequence of filmed events, the direct and delayed launching events were reversed by switching the projector to run backwards. As predicted, the group of infants who had watched the direct launching increased their looking to the reversed sequence more than the group who had watched the delayed reaction.

According to Leslie and Keeble, infants are sensitive to causal relations and can discriminate causal from spatio-temporal relations. As part of a modular organisation of the perceptual system that operates in the absence of prior relevant knowledge, the early perception of causal relations may lay the foundation for the later development of causal understanding.

CHANGING VIEWS OF CHILDREN'S KNOWLEDGE: A WORKING MODEL

Piaget often examined child development through observing infants' reaching strategies or interviewing preschoolers and primary school children. On this basis, he mounted a case for early conceptual limitations. Alternatively, the child might be understood in the manner of a young philosopher who cannot yet express his or her intelligence in motor development or through the use of vocabulary. The British short story author Roald Dahl (1959) writes of the case of a philosopher who had died. However, his brain has been preserved and remains attached to an eye.

The philosopher retains his knowledge of the world and his earthly pretences (for example, to read newspapers such as *The Times* of London). Yet he cannot speak and the only way he can communicate is by moving the pupil of his eye up and down.

The infant, unable to speak, immature in its physical growth, and susceptible to long periods of sleep, may still have a capacity to understand that is closer to Dahl's philosopher than to Piaget's extreme notion of a very young creature who lacks a concept of objects. Indeed, the physical immaturity of infants influences their participation in experiments in the first place. To secure a sample for a study often requires that two or more infants must be tested for every one infant that can be included in the results. For instance, as reported by Bertoncini et al. (1988, p. 25) in one of their experiments on infants' representations of speech sounds, it was necessary to test 174 infants to obtain a sample of 48 (mean age = 10.2 weeks). Many of the excluded infants cried, while others fell asleep or ceased to give a sucking response during the course of the experiment.

Nevertheless, although we cannot attribute anything like full-blown knowledge to infants (and do not assume that they can read newspapers), at least judging from those who can and do participate in experiments, they are far more precocious than Piaget originally described. Their "Dahl-like" abilities stand in opposition to Piaget's contention that they lack object permanence as well as to the belief of William James (1890/1960) that the world of infants is one of "blooming buzzing confusion".

The list of infants' achievements in experiments is extensive. They can make connections between touch, sound, and vision. They can identify voices and their attention is captured by objects that are made to disappear. They perceive differences in number, and would appear to be sensitive to causal relations. All of this underscores their ability to represent the world, and points to the early existence of a capacity or mental "architecture" for dealing with abstract concepts. They may have an inborn set of functions that can be recombined in subtle ways during the first year of life to analyse phenomena such as number and object relations.

Of course, with increasing age, infants become more aware in their analysis of changing situations (Mandler, 1987). Yet the use of techniques of habituation and recovery of interest has yielded a more genuine appraisal of knowledge in infancy. The parallel with questioning children in experiments is clear: should conversation be seen as irrelevant or redundant, children may be misled to answer incorrectly. They may in turn mislead the adult into believing that they are inherently limited in their conceptual development. In this way, a well-meaning methodology can obscure an appreciation of development and instead inadvertently produce cases of "misleading children".

By virtue of his experimental results, Piaget (1972, p. 49) termed the issue of how to speed up developmental processes in order to move children into a more advanced stage as the "American dilemma". This approach is certainly in line with the (brash?) proposition that potential genius can be discovered very early and accelerated. However, an uncritical acceptance of Piaget's position can distract educators from legitimate concerns about children's potential.

My point in this excursion into recent research on infancy is that even very young children are equipped with an abstract understanding. To make sense of the world, they have "storage drawers" of knowledge—a set of functions—that structure their thinking and behaviour. Infant research indicates that the dilemma of how to treat the early potential of children must be taken seriously and cannot be dismissed as preposterous. It raises several questions about the existence of conceptual limitations in child development. To what extent can infants become preschoolers who do not have the ability to think abstractly about number, causality, objects, and persons? Can so many primary school children have the same lack of ability? The evidence from experiments on infants provides grounds to hypothesise answers. With carefully conceived but simple experiments, it is possible to uncover pre-existing knowledge on tasks requiring abstract concepts. That is not to say that children actually use the correct, or best, abstract strategies to solve problems, only that they often have the capacity to do so. To support this capacity, attention is required on how the conversational world of children differs from that of adults.

The working model of development which emerges is that young children have a substantial *implicit* knowledge or conceptual competence. This may not be revealed because the measures designed to test children require procedural or language interpretation skills that are beyond their grasp or experience. On many tasks, they may lack plans or procedures to translate their understanding into performance even though they have at least an implicit, skeletal knowledge of the correct response. However, even if children do have these procedures, they need to share adults' use of conversational rules to interpret the meaning and purpose of questions in the way intended by the investigator. Too often, experimenters' models of child development have taken these assumptions largely for granted. Therefore, it is important to consider the nature of conversation with children.

If development is not necessarily restricted by conceptual limitations in the manner proposed by Piaget, an alternative account is needed for young children's lack of success in experiments. The model proposed here is that children frequently can succeed on measures of their abstract understanding if these are formulated in a "child-friendly" language. Support for my position that their weak performance on standard developmental measures can often be explained in terms of their interpretation of adults' use of conversational rules comes from a variety of sources: work on children's number and measurement abilities (discussed in Chapter Two), experiments on their ability to detect causal relations and to represent objects and viewpoints (Chapters Three and Four), studies of friendship, popularity, and concepts of gender (Chapter Five), and research on the understanding of authority and the acquisition of academic skills (Chapter Six). This evidence (summarised in Chapter Seven) has significance for education and child care. What follows is an examination of how children appreciate the meaning and purpose of the questions put to them.

2 Communication With Children On Number and Measurement Problems

CONSERVATION AS A THEORETICAL BUILDING BLOCK

Probably the most famous demonstration of young children's capacity for understanding has come from conservation experiments. For Piaget (1952; 1970), children under approximately 7 years are non-conservers; they judge transformed quantities by focusing on perceptual changes in appearance rather than on features that remain invariant such as number. Suppose they are given two rows of six buttons, each arranged on a one-to-one correspondence. An experimenter asks if the two rows have the same amount and children ordinarily respond that the rows are the same. The rows are then transformed so that one is now shorter and denser than the other. The question is asked again. Non-conservers say that the numbers are unequal and may choose the row which is longer. According to the Piagetian interpretation, they lack an understanding of "invariance", the concept that quantities remain the same despite perceptual changes. This is evidence for a preoperational stage of development. At the age of approximately 7 years, children now correctly conserve and enter into a stage of concrete operations.

However, 60 years ago, Piaget (1929) in his book *The Child's Conception of the World* wrote of difficulties in asking children questions. To promote the diagnosis of authentic reasoning abilities, his rule was to encourage "the flow of spontaneous tendencies" in advocating that "every symptom" of the child's thought should be placed in its "mental context". Questions ideally should be asked in the manner and form of the spon-

15

taneous questions actually asked by children of the same age and under. In efforts to avoid "systematic errors" inherent in the "pure experiment" in which children may give artificial responses, Piaget was particularly concerned with the effect of repeated questioning and lengthy interviewing. He sought to deal with this problem by presenting counter-suggestions (i.e., "Another child told me that the two rows still had the same"), to let the child talk for a few minutes and return to the subject indirectly later, and to pursue the connection with the child's other convictions. He advocated that the interviewer probe the roots of the suspect answer and then ask the question in as many different ways as possible. But while he believed that "suggestion may thus be avoided by means of patience and analysis", Piaget (1929, pp. 27–28) did concede a "much more serious difficulty": "that of distinguishing from among the results of the examination the point to be regarded as the child's original contribution and that due to previous adult influences." This problem is of crucial importance in experiments on child development but was never squarely confronted, let alone resolved, in Piaget's research programme. His attempts to come squarely to grips with this issue were rather casual.

Nevertheless, although it is not easy to determine how children answer questions in the way that they do, there is a first theoretical leap in research based on Piaget's approach. Using a form of "clinical method" consisting of interviews with children, Piaget and his followers have interpreted the results of conservation studies to illustrate that young children centre on perceptual aspects of transformations and ignore invariant features. They cannot compensate by integrating information from two or more dimensions of a problem. For example, they do not take into account density as well as length in comparing the numbers of candies or counters set out in parallel rows and often judge that the longer row has more irrespective of its number. If water is poured from a short, wide beaker into a longer, narrow one, they determine the amount often by focusing on one dimension only (i.e., height) rather than compensating with another (i.e., width). In this respect, Piaget concluded that children are "egocentric" and cannot consider more than one dimension or point of view in making judgements of physical quantity.

A second leap in the argument comes when applying children's lack of success on measures of cognitive development such as conservation to theories of social development. If they are egocentric and cannot conserve, then what are the implications for their friendships and their ability to consider others' points of view? Further, what are the implications for sex-role concepts that require the conservation of gender attributes across superficial perceptual transformations in dress? For example, do boys think that they will turn into girls if they wear girls' clothing, or do they believe that gender is invariant and is unrelated to dress style? As will be seen in Chapters Five and Six, many writers (including myself) have at one time or another maintained that cognitive development as described by Piaget is a prerequisite for concepts of friendship and gender.

These two leaps are implicit in Piagetian research on social development. Problematic though it is, interpreters of Piaget have taken a third leap: that education should be matched to children's stage of development or, at least, delayed until they have attained the "cognitive prerequisites" to demonstrate a readiness to acquire academic skills such as arithmetic as well as to understand others' viewpoints.

This chapter concerns the critical first leap that young children genuinely share the purpose underlying questions on cognitive tasks such as measures of conservation and that their incorrect responses are not simply due to the language of the experiment. The assumption has gained considerable acceptance in much neo-Piagetian research on cognitive development and has provided a theoretical foundation for work in social development (the second leap) and education (the third leap). For example, in his generally thought-provoking and well-written textbook, Robert Siegler (1986, p. 3) introduces a discussion of how children process information by referring to an often cited study by DeVries:

> Some of the most interesting parts of children's thinking are the parts where children differ most markedly from adults. DeVries (1969) provided a particularly compelling example of such a difference. She was interested in 3- to 6-year-olds' understanding of the difference between appearance and reality. The children were presented with an unusually sweet-tempered cat named Maynard and were allowed to pet him. When the experimenter asked what Maynard was, all of them knew he was a cat. Then the experimenter put a mask on Maynard's head, in plain sight of the children. The mask was that of a fierce-looking dog. The experimenter asked, "Look, it has a face like a dog. What is this animal now?" DeVries found that many of the 3-year-olds (unlike the 6-year-olds) thought that Maynard had become a dog. They refused to pet him and said that under his skin he had a dog's bones and a dog's stomach.

According to Siegler, "It is simply stunning that a human being, even a very young one, would think that a cat could turn into a dog." While he cautions that differences between the responses of 3-year-olds and older children should not be overemphasised and that young children display adult-like abilities in many situations, no consideration is given to another possibility. Children at 3 years-of-age have little experience in conversations with adults. Instead of assuming that an experimenter wishes to discover what children know about the distinction between the appearance of an animal and its true identity, they may seek to comply with the perceived force of the question. Rather than reveal their authentic conservation of the identity of animals despite superficial perceptual changes, they may seek to flatter an adult for an entertaining display. (Perhaps, we may add, "it is simply stunning" that adults would so uncritically accept, in a serious model of development, that young children believe that a cat could turn into a dog.)

EXPERIMENTS AND LANGUAGE: CONSERVATION OF NUMBER AS A STARTING POINT

In contemporary critiques of research on cognitive development, the issue of "demand characteristics" inherent in the conservation experiment has not gone unnoticed. In an incisive pair of exploratory studies with 6-year-olds, Rose and Blank (1974) tested the hypothesis that non-conservation is influenced by the language used in the experiment—specifically, that repetition of the question (e.g., "Are there the same number in both rows or does one row have more?") misleads children to change their answers and respond incorrectly. Rose and Blank found that children gave significantly more conservation responses when only one question was asked after the rows had been transformed than in a standard two-question condition. This is similar to the effect we see in adult conversations where repeated questioning (for example, "How are you?" Response: "OK." Repeated question, "How are you?") results in response switching or, perhaps in some cases, annoyance at having to repeat the answer. However, Rose and Blank's findings have met with equivocal support in replication studies (for example, Neilson, Dockrell, & McKechnie, 1983; Samuel & Bryant, 1984) and, in any event, were largely restricted to 6-year-olds' judgements of small numbers of items.

Because conservation has become such a theoretically key issue, it requires a fresh investigation. There are experiments that can be carried out to consider whether children's failure on conservation problems is due to a deep limitation in understanding or to the nature of a methodology that can provoke children to respond inconsistently. To address this problem, we examined children's appreciation of repeated questioning in experiments with 4-, 5-, and 6-year-olds (Siegal, Waters, & Dinwiddy, 1988). As in most of our experiments, the children came from middle-class areas of Brisbane, located near the University of Queensland. Our conservation project was designed with two purposes: (1) to examine children's responses using a one-question procedure on forms of conservation length tasks; and (2) to determine their attributions for conservation and non-conservation answers in one-question and two-question conditions.

A total of 180 children participated in our Experiment One. Within each age group, half were randomly assigned to a condition where they were tested by a one-question procedure, and half to the traditional or standard two-question testing condition often used by Piagetians.

The children were shown two displays each consisting of two parallel rows of buttons. Each row consisted of 20 buttons 1cm in diameter. The display used for the standard testing condition consisted of rows of pink and purple buttons. For the one-question condition, rows of red and blue buttons were used. The initial (Array A) and post-transformation (Array B) location of the buttons for both displays are shown in Fig. 2.1.

Why would we use two rows of 20 buttons? As other have noted (for example, Halford & Boyle, 1985), these numbers preclude the use of counting as a problem-solving strategy. The numbers and positions of the counters also avoid the possibility that children could make judgements by a kind of default strategy should one of the rows appear more salient before a transformation; when asked initially to identify which row has

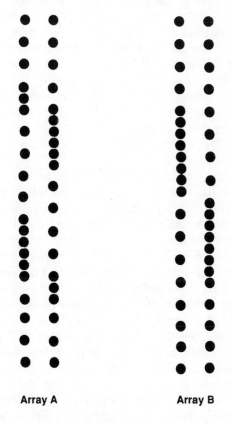

Array A   **Array B**

FIG. 2.1   The two arrays used in the first conservation of number experiment (from Siegal, Waters, & Dinwiddy, 1988).

more, children's choice of row was at a chance level of 50%. Therefore, the displays provided a simple test of consistency in their judgements under one-question and standard conditions of numbers in rows that have been perceptually rearranged but remain the same with nothing added or taken away.

To record pre-transformation judgements, the children were given a small fliptop box containing pairs of buttons (either red and blue or purple and pink, matched according to the testing condition). Each child was given "two trials": one trial on each display in which Array A was transformed into B. Half the children in each age group first received the standard condition and the other half received the one-question condition.

In the standard condition, the displays were placed directly in front of the child who was seated at a table opposite a female experimenter. The child was told: "Here are two big rows of buttons." This row has pink buttons in it and this row has purple buttons in it. Point to the row which has more buttons." The order of mention of the rows was alternated on successive standard trials as was the original left or right positioning of each row in the display. The child was then given the box containing the pairs of buttons and told: "You think the purple (or pink) row has more. So take that (colour) button from the box and hold it in your hand. Now watch carefully what I'm doing." The experimenter rearranged the rows, alternatively transforming the left and right row first on subsequent trials. Then she repeated the request to "point to the row which has more buttons" and asked the child, "Did you pick the pink (or purple) row before? Let's see. What's in your hand?"

In the one-question condition, the child was told to "think about which row (blue or red) has more buttons. But don't tell. If you think the blue row has more, take that button from the box. If you think the red row has more, take that button from the box. But don't show me. Hide it in your hand." Again, both the order of mention and left or right positioning of the rows was alternated on successive one-question trials. After the child chose a button privately, the experimenter transformed the array. The child was asked to compare the rows and reveal his or her initial selection of button as in the standard condition. No feedback was given on responses.

Conservation judgements under each of the two testing conditions for the three age groups, together with the numbers of children who conserved on both trials, are shown in Table 2.1. As predicted, the children tested on the first trial under the one-question condition gave significantly more conservation judgements on this trial than did those tested under the standard condition. Given the criterion for successful conservation of consistent judgements before and after the counters were rearranged, 78% of all the children tested under the one-question condition could be considered conservers: 63% of the 4-year-olds, 77% of the 5-year-olds, and 93% of the 6-year-olds. By contrast, only 23% of those tested under the

TABLE 2.1
Numbers of Correct Responses in the First Experiment on Conservation of
Number (From Siegal, Waters, & Dinwiddy, 1988). In Each Condition,
There Were 30 Children From Each Age Group

	Group		
Condition	4 Years	5 Years	6 Years
One-question (trial 1)	19	23	28
Standard (trial 2)	16	19	23
Conserved on both trials	13	17	23
Standard (trial 1)	5	6	10
One-question (trial 2)	10	13	21
Conserved on both trials	3	4	10

standard condition on the first trial reached this criterion.

On the second trial, as expected, more conservation judgements were given in the standard format if one question instead of two questions had been asked in the first trial. For each of the three groups, performance under the one-question condition was impaired by experience in the first trial with the standard procedure.

Significantly more children in each age group conserved on both trials when tested first in the one-question condition than in the standard one. By this criterion, 59% of all children tested in the one-question condition followed by the standard were classifiable as conservers compared to only 19% of those tested in the reverse order. Of the children who conserved on the first trial, 67% of the 4-year-olds, 72% of the 5-year-olds, and 87% of the 6-year-olds conserved on the second trial, indicating that the answers of the children who did conserve were unlikely to be random. Therefore, as in the studies of Rose and Blank (1974), the one-question condition elicited significantly more conservation (i.e., consistent) answers than did the standard two-question condition. Moreover, prior experience with the one-question procedure enhanced subsequent performance on a standard trial, suggesting that it served to clarify the requirements of the task.

However, there are two possible objections to the interpretation that the children in Experiment One were giving consistent, conservation answers. First, those tested by the one-question procedure may have desired to share their secretive button choice with the experimenter. Rather than conserving, they may have merely repeated their initial choice when the post-transformation request for a response was made. Second, some children tested in the one-question condition may have offered per-severated judgements since no other perceptual bases for post-transformational judgements were available.

In our Experiment Two, we sought to rule out these possibilities by asking children to make attributions for others' performance under one- and two-question conditions. Recognising that attributions for the performance of others are not the same as attributions for one's own performance, our aim was straightforward: it was to test further the hypothesis that they interpret repeated questioning to require that the initial answer should be switched.

Following the method used in several earlier studies (Fluck & Hewison, 1979; Gelman & Meck, 1983), we asked children to evaluate the answers of puppets in a detection task. The puppets were shown as subjects in videotaped conservation experiments. The children's task was to give causal attributions for the puppets' responses. If children interpret a repeated request as a cue to change answers, they should assign "external" attributions (for example, "to please someone else") to puppets' lack of conservation in the standard two-question condition, and "internal" attributions (for example, "really thought was true") to conservation responses or, possibly, to non-conservation in a one-question condition.

There were 32 children in our Experiment Two. Each one was initially alerted to the possibility that choices can be made to please others by instructions derived from Asch's (1958) classic series of conformity experiments. The experimenter read two stories to the children. These contained two practice requests for attributions. For example:

> Sally was playing with a few of her friends at kindergarten when the teacher came up to the children and showed them two blocks, one big and one small. The teacher asked each child to point to the biggest block. The first child pointed to the smaller block, and so did the others. Then it was Sally's turn. She pointed to that block too. Do you think Sally pointed to the small block because (a) she really wanted to please the other children and be like them or because (b) she really thought that block was the biggest? (All the children chose "a".)
>
> The teacher showed the same blocks to another group of children who were playing with Louise, and asked them to point to the smallest block. The first child pointed to the big block, and so did the others. Then it was Louise's turn. She pointed to the other block instead. Do you think Louise pointed to the small block because (a) she wanted to please the other children or because (b) she really thought it was the smallest block? (All the children chose "b".)
>
> So you see, sometimes people do things just to please others, and sometimes they do things because they really think what they do is true.

The children then viewed four videotaped segments depicting the answers of puppets on the conservation of number arrays used in the first study. The puppets were shown tested by a female experimenter, twice under one-question conditions and twice under standard conditions. For the two segments in each condition, one puppet was a conserver and the other one was a non-conserver. The presentation order of the segments was varied systematically.

After viewing each segment, the children were asked if the puppet had responded "just to please the grown-up" or "the way the puppet really thought was true", representing external and internal attributions respectively. They were then required to indicate the certainty of his or her choice by pointing to one of three triangles of increasing size representing "not sure at all" (smallest triangle), "half sure" (middle-sized triangle) and "very sure" (largest triangle). All children had used the scale correctly in sample cases given in the instructions. Ratings were given scores ranging from 0 to 5. A response of "very sure, internal" was scored as 0 and one "very sure, external" was scored as 5. "Half sure, internal", "not at all sure, internal", "not at all sure, external", and "half sure, external", were scored as 1, 2, 3 and 4 points respectively.

For puppets' non-conservation responses in the standard condition, the percentage of children's external choices—"just to please the grown-up"—amounted to 69% and was significantly above a chance level. Only in this condition did they give external attribution ratings (mean of 3.47 out of a maximum possible 5.00). The percentage of external choices was below chance level at 25% for conservation response in the standard condition and at 28% for responses in the one-question condition. Attributions for non-conservation in the one-question condition where the children had no clear basis for inferring causality, either through correct responses or repeated questioning, were at a chance level of 44%.

Experiments like these require qualifications. Since the objective was to examine children's consistency under repeated questioning and to avoid their use of counting and other extraneous problem-solving strategies, our conservation tasks departed somewhat from those originally used by Piaget (1952). Moreover, we must note that no necessary connection exists between children's own answers on conservation tasks and their attributions for others' responses. In the first experiment, a minority of children, especially 4-year-olds, did not conserve and, in the second experiment, there were some who did not give external attributions for others' non-conservation answers in the traditional, two-question format. Although repeated questioning may jeopardise children's performance on many tasks, asking only one question does not guarantee that all will respond correctly.

Bearing these considerations in mind, our results are in agreement with Rose and Blank's original findings and were replicated in two subsequent experiments on conservation of length where preschoolers could indicate that a straight line and a line bent into the shape of a cresent were the same length (Siegal, Waters, & Dinwiddy, 1988, Experiments Three and Four).

As illustrated in Fig. 2.2, there is striking similarity between children's attributions for puppets' responses in conservation of number and length experiments.

Therefore, while children are often able to respond correctly in standard, two-question conservation of number or length experiments, they may change their answers because they are prompted to do so by repeated questioning. The majority give external causal attributions for non-conserving responses in the standard procedure. By contrast, they con-

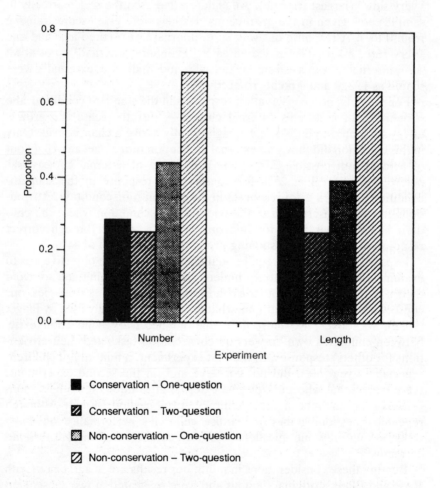

FIG. 2.2 Proportion of children's external causal choices for puppets' responses in conservation of number and length experiments (from Siegal, Waters, & Dinwiddy, 1988).

serve and give internal causal attributions in a one-question condition. These results do not offer direct support for the proposition that unsuccessful performance in *individual* children is due to repeated questioning, but they provide data to entertain this hypothesis as entirely plausible. As a *group*, children's apparent lack of understanding on conservation measures is strongly influenced by repeated questioning.

EXPLANATIONS FOR PERFORMANCE

This is only one illustration of how at least some children may be misled by the questions asked in experiments. It establishes that their non-conserving (or inconsistent) responses on measures of cognitive development can be influenced by their interpretation of the experimenter's intent. Through repeated questioning, adults can mislead children to give inconsistent answers. These answers in turn mislead adults to accept a theory of cognitive development that does not faithfully reflect the depth of children's understanding. Such interactions support the model of development which proposes that children's knowledge is obscured by a clash of conversational worlds.

One scenario of non-conservation under the standard two-question procedure is illustrated in Fig. 2.3. However, there are several, more specific explanations that lead to hypotheses for children's answers to questioning forms which stray from conversational rules.

Explanation One: Switching Under Uncertainty

According to this explanation which was favoured by Rose and Blank, repeated questioning misleads children to provide inconsistent answers by implying that the first answer was not acceptable and should be switched. Hence, repeated questioning misleads children to provide inconsistent responses. Since problems that require judgements of number and length can contain language factors that affect communication, clarification of instructions should facilitate performance.

Consistent with this explanation, Schiff (1983) has maintained that children as young as 3½ years can conserve length where care has been taken to avoid linguistic confusion, and Rochel Gelman (1982; Gelman & Gallistel, 1978, pp. 13–14) has claimed that 3-year-olds rapidly acquire number conservation responses in training studies designed to clarify the nature of the task.

For example, Gelman (1982) attempted to illustrate 3-year-olds' ability to conserve number by directing their attention to toy turtles in rows placed in one-to-one correspondence. The children were asked to count

FIG. 2.3   An illustration of the possible context of non-conservation answers.

the number of items in one of the rows. The row was then covered and the children were asked, "How many are under my hands?" The question was repeated for the other row. When one of the rows was transformed, the children now retained their initial response and conserved. Yet although this procedure might have uncovered a pre-existing but fragile understanding, there is the possibility that the children did not genuinely conserve and did not understand that the same number remained regardless of the transformation. This procedure might have simply signalled to the children that it is all right to give the correct (or same) answer.

More recently, Gelman, Meck, and Merkin (1986) have suggested that repeated requests on counting tasks underestimate children's numerical competence, and have maintained that preschoolers' counting mistakes under repeated or ambiguous instructions reflect an inexperience at "stepping outside a particular interpretation of an utterance and selecting another" (p. 27). Consider the example of an adult's comment such as "Did you get a haircut?" that immediately follows a child's haircut. Although it is obvious that the child did receive a haircut and, in this sense, the comment is irrelevant, preschoolers may not be easily able to attribute to the adult an alternative motive of sarcasm or sauciness (see, for example, Ackerman, 1981). They may be puzzled or unsettled by the lack of co-operation shown by the adult in commenting upon what is obviously the case.

As Gelman and her colleagues have maintained, children's responses to repeated questioning may reflect a lack of experience or confidence in the answer. Similarly, Hughes (1986, p. 46) has claimed that uncertainty underlies responses on simple arithmetic problems. He gives an example from an interview with a child called Amanda (3 years, 11 months):

> MH: *How many is two and one?* (Long pause. No response.) *Well how many bricks is two bricks and one brick?*
> Amanda: *Three.*
> MH: *Okay. So how many is two and one?*
> Amanda: (Pause.) *Four?* (Hesitantly.)
> MH: *How many is one brick and one more brick?*
> Amanda: *Two bricks.*
> MH: *So how many is one and one?*
> Amanda: *One, maybe.*

According to Hughes, "Amanda clearly saw no connection between the questions concerned with bricks and the more abstract questions—indeed, she seems to be using a strategy of giving a different response to the latter. It is as if she is thinking, "Well, I don't understand this question, but I know it's not the same as the previous one, so I'll try a different answer.""

Explanation Two: Insincerity

An alternative explanation for children's lack of success is that, in at least some cases, they are certain of the answers after all. Yet they may not state their convictions because of unfavourable perceptions of the experimenter's questioning or the task itself.

For example, Perner, Leekam, and Wimmer (1986) have suggested that, because young children know that the experimenter already knows the answer, they regard standard conservation questions as insincere. Their incorrect responses reflect an insufficient analysis of a well-meaning experimenter's reason for asking the same question twice rather than an inability to conserve. When told to give their response to a second, naive experimenter who had not heard their first answer, the majority of 4- to 6-year-olds now conserve. Older children have a more advanced appreciation of intentions in conversations. They conserve in any event because they can understand the "second order epistemic intention" of the experimenter—that he or she wants to know whether children know. To account for non-conservation, Perner and his co-workers substitute an inability in early childhood to understand the mind of the experimenter for the lack of a logical ability to disregard perceptual appearances. (This may be rather strong. Instead of an inability to understand the mind of the experimenter it may simply be inexperience in knowing others' intentions. See Chapter Four.)

Therefore, care must be taken to prevent an uncritical acceptance of the conclusion that non-conservation answers are necessarily due to an uncertain conceptual understanding. Under prolonged or repeated questioning some children may not grow less confident of the answer. They only change their response because of the perceived insincerity of the experimenter or the unattractive nature of the task. As it happens, conservation problems may not capture the hearts and minds of young children. A quick finish may allow a return to more attractive activities. Even if repeated questioning is avoided, children may regard some tasks as unattractive and respond in ways that do not provide insight into their authentic understanding.

Explanation Three: The Overattractive Task

Explanations One and Two dwell on the more negative aspects of questioning children in interviews. However, language explanations for why children do not display the depth of their understanding may take a more positive tone. For example, a task may in fact be too attractive, particularly if the answer seems obvious. Preschoolers can interpret certain forms of questioning to require age-typical or "cute" answers, whereas older children, who see themselves more as adults, do not interpret questioning in this way. An example that may fit this explanation comes from research on children's gender concepts or "conservation" of gender (see Chapter Five).

Explanation Four: Trust in the Experimenter

These possibilities do not exhaust reasons for why children's lack of success on cognitive tasks may not reflect a conceptual limitation. Yet another explanation involves the naive approach to the task which can be seen in terms of a "trust in the experimenter" hypothesis. An example that fits this explanation comes from research on children's conceptions of contagion and contamination in which children must understand that adults could offer them a contaminated drink in order to determine their knowledge of the causes of illness (see Chapter Three).

Explanation Five: Word-use

A fifth explanation is that children's lack of success merely indicates cases in which they do not share how adults use words. This interpretation has a long history. It has been argued that preschoolers cannot easily be granted an understanding of words such as "more", "less", and "same" (Donaldson & Balfour, 1968). More recently, Cummins, Kintsch, Reusser, and Weimer (1988) have proposed that primary schoolers' difficulties with word arithmetic problems (e.g., "Mary has three marbles. John has four marbles more than Mary. How many marbles does John have?") are due to their misunderstanding of the uses of words such as "some" and "altogether" and linguistic forms such as "How many more X's than Y's?" Problems with word uses do not provide a full explanation of children's apparent inability to understand abstract concepts. But the hypothesis has been far from adequately exploited (see Chapter Six).

TOWARDS THE ADJUDICATION OF ALTERNATIVE EXPLANATIONS

In cognitive science, a useful distinction has often been made between a symbolic representation of goals, beliefs, and knowledge and the "functional architecture"—a metaphor derived from computer research—required to interpret the symbols into meaning (Pylyshyn, 1984, pp. 30–31). Two people whose beliefs and goals are the same may be functionally distinguishable if they have, for example, different memory retrieval mechanisms or degrees of alertness.

In Piaget's analysis, children and adults share beliefs about the purpose of comparisons in experiments. Age differences in conservation answers are due to differences in the schema or functional architecture required to use concepts such as invariance in number. Young children are at a preoperational stage. In adapting to the environment, they later come to share the same logic and concepts as adults. By contrast, the results of our conservation tasks suggest that adults and children may often have similar logic and concepts but differ on the nature of the language used in the experiment. Rather than sharing the experimenter's purpose, children may be anticipating that they should give particular answers. They may be uncomfortable with the task in the first place and be induced to respond incorrectly, or they may be confident and know the answer but respond incorrectly because they read insincerity into the motives of the experimenter. Alternatively, even if they do understand the experimenter's purpose, they may give incorrect answers to seek attention or to shorten or prolong the experiment.

Piaget's clinical interview method does not circumvent these alternative explanations. Consequently, children's beliefs about conservation—even if these do turn out to be rather fragile—may actually be no different than those of adults. In this respect, adults and children may be functionally indistinguishable. However, adults and children may differ in their beliefs about the meaning of words or the purpose underlying repeated or unconventional questioning. Therefore, children may respond in a seemingly illogical manner.

As Carey (1985b, p. 200) points out, the specification of an initial state of cognitive development is a prerequisite for a theory of learning. A description of the child's initial state must come before or proceed together with an examination of mechanisms of change. A major distinction that can be drawn here is between the child's capacity to use concepts such as invariance in number, and knowing when to employ them. Children's "initial state" as shown in experimental contexts may reflect not so much their lack of ability to use abstract concepts but their interpretation of the experimenter's intent in communication.

In everyday conversations, young children often adjust their speech to suit the characteristics of the listener (Shatz & Gelman, 1973). Moreover, they are skilled in comprehending the motives of a speaker (Braine & Rumain, 1983). They assume that a speaker's messages will be motivated by co-operativeness, non-redundancy, truthfulness, relevance, and clarity—conventions of communication that hve been noted by philosophers of language. These are rational, systematic rules that "constrain" our conversations. For example, to communicate effectively, speakers should contribute no more and no less information than is required. They should contribute that which they believe to be true and avoid saying what they believe to be false or that for which adequate evidence is lacking. They should be relevant and avoid ambiguity and obscurity of expression.

In his exposition of speech conventions, Grice (1975, p. 45), a philosopher, formally states a "co-operative principle" that underlies effective communication: "Make your conversational contribution such as is required at the stage at which it occurs, by the accepted purpose or direction of the talk exchange in which you are engaged." To produce conservation that is in accordance with this principle, he lists four rules or maxims that may be described, briefly, as the maxims of quantity: "Speak no more or no less than is required"; quality: "Try to speak the truth and avoid falsehood"; relevance (or relation): "Be relevant and informative"; and manner: "Avoid obscurity and ambiguity". (There are a number of complexities in the study of pragmatics in language; critiques of Grice's approach are offered by Brown & Levinson, 1987; Cohen, 1971; Leech, 1983; and Sperber & Wilson, 1986). These maxims can be called the "conversational rules".

In conversations between adults, it is mutually understood that the rules may sometimes be explicitly flouted to create what Grice has termed "conversational implicatures". These non-conventional forms of language are used, for example, where the rules clash (e.g., in cases where to be informative would violate the rule to speak no more than is required), or where irony is intended through a statement of the obvious, or where there is a desire motivated by politeness to ensure that the listener understands through repeated questioning. However, even in conversations between adults, the listener is liable to be misled if a rule is quietly broken.

For the most part, preschoolers aged 4 years abide by conversational rules. In soliciting answers to questions, they co-operatively adjust their speech to suit the characteristics of the listener (Gelman & Shatz, 1977). They speak in less sophisticated ways to children younger than themselves and use more complicated forms of language when conversing with adults.

Yet contrary to the rules to be relevant and to speak no more than is required, an experimenter may pose questions where the answer is obvious or repeat questions when an answer has already been given. Young children may not recognise that the purpose underlying departures from conversational rules is to establish their understanding of concepts. Instead, they may act on a mistaken implicature and assume that, for example, repeated questioning implies a rejection of their first answer and is an invitation to switch the second time around regardless of whether that answer was correct. Moreover, contrary to the quality and manner rules to be truthful and avoid ambiguity and obscurity, children can be asked questions that require them to be sceptical of the experimenter's sincerity or to share the use of certain key words. Again, they may respond incorrectly not because they do not know the answer but because they misinterpret the experimenter's purpose or use of language. In some cases, communication may be jeopardised by their perception that the experimenter is not even observing the basic principle that speakers co-operate with the listener.

The communication gulf between adults and young children can be illustrated by comic incidents in conversations between adults. Take an example from the Marx Brothers where one adult says to another, "Where can I get hold of you?" and the response is, "I don't know. I'm ticklish all over!" This gulf in misperceiving the experimenter's intent in questioning is probably more pervasive in adult–child communication. But it is also more subtle since children are less experienced in conversation and may have difficulty in blocking out an implicature that the experimenter did not intend. Furthermore, compared to adults, they may be less likely to retort spontaneously in response to questions and to offer repairs for improving communication. For instance, recall Piaget's method of using counter-suggestions to probe for certainty in answers: to tell children that another child has said the opposite. By contrast, children may not share the experimenter's purpose. They may extract meaning from their personal knowledge of others and strain to import the own relevance; their response to such a suggestion may be tacitly based on the presumed answer to the question, "Is he a dumb or smart kid?"

SPONTANEOUSLY DECIDING WHICH ONE HAS MORE

The watershed between "knowing how", or at least having the "capacity to know how", and "knowing when" to apply a strategy for solving a problem remains at the crux of cognitive development. It is not enough to give a child a particular problem, record failure, and then conclude that the child does not know how. It can only be ventured that he or she might not share the experimenter's purpose or use of language in questioning. Once this purpose and language is shared, children can be shown when to apply an appropriate strategy. A good example comes from the studies of children's measurement abilities.

According to Piaget (Piaget, Inhelder, & Szeminska, 1964), children under approximately the age of 7 years are unable to use a measuring device to compare the length of objects. They are not capable of inferring that an intervening measure such as a stick or rod can be used to check the heights of two towers of blocks set on stands at different levels.

Bryant and Kopytynska (1976) challenged this position. They reasoned that young children's apparent inability to use measurement devices is not due to the absence of some underlying conceptual mechanism. Rather, children often do not recognise when these devices need to be used. To succeed on measurement tasks, they need to know that a direct comparison by eye is unreliable and that a measurement device is required. In Bryant and Kopytynska's studies, 5- and 6-year-olds accurately compared the depth of holes in blocks of wood after an experimenter pointed out the presence of a measuring rod. Therefore, children may indeed have the necessary skill to make inferences but at times they do not always realise when this skill is needed.

My analysis of children's understanding of the conservation task is in agreement with these results. There are many explanations for non-conservation that can be framed in terms of a gap in communication between children and experimenters. Children may have the skill to conserve quantities but, caught in this gap, the skill is not translated into success. Bryant (1985) further contends that young children's difficulties in the addition and subtraction of quantities are rooted not so much in their lack of mathematical ability but in the realisation that certain number skills are required. Children may need to be shown that concepts of number have a function in solving problems.

Possibly there is some biologically or maturationally influenced upper bound in children's capacity to process information on cognitive tasks (see, for example, Case, 1985, pp. 377–381). Yet despite similarities in maturation, children vary greatly in their performance. Moreover, apparently rapid changes in their information-processing ability might turn out to be a byproduct of rapid changes in their responses to requests using unconventional forms of language that violate Grice's rules or maxims for communication in conversations. For this reason, the first purpose in experiments must be to describe the initial state or "know-how" in children's cognition. A next step is to find procedures by which this state can develop.

RECOVERING FORMERLY OBSCURED CAPACITY IN CONTEMPORARY DEVELOPMENTAL RESEARCH

During the 1980s, many psychologists have sought to recast Piaget's findings on cognitive development into a somewhat different theoretical orientation. Two of these efforts seem especially noteworthy: the studies of Siegler (1981) and Flavell, Flavell, and Green (1983). The former approach characterises children's inability to conserve number in terms of "rule-complexity"; the latter involves their knowledge of the distinction between perceptual appearance and "reality" (i.e., the invariant properties of objects).

Using a novel approach in experiments with children aged 3 to 9 years, Siegler attempted to characterise development in terms of an acquisition of increasingly powerful rules for problem solving. Unlike Piaget, his "rule-assessment" approach does not often presume a structured whole or similarity in children's performance across different tasks that amounts to a conceptual limitation. To some extent, it also recognises that tasks which reduce children's dependence on language comprehension provide a clearer indication of their understanding than responses in a Piagetian interview. However, it steers clear of the need to consider conversational rules.

According to Siegler, children's ability on number conservation problems can be interpreted as involving the acquisition of four rules:

1. Rule I in which children concentrate on the dominant dimension (i.e., the length of the rows).
2. Rule II where they also consider the subordinate dimension (i.e., row density) when values on the dominant one are equal.
3. Rule III in which they consider both dimensions but do not know how to resolve conflicts between the two.
4. Rule IV when conservation is obtained.

Thus at Rule I, children are able to solve problems involving rows of counters with density held constant by focusing on the dominant dimension of length. At Rule II, they can focus on density with length held constant. Children at Rule III consider both density and length but cannot consider conflicts such as between a row of four matched with a shorter, denser row of five.

While Siegler found mixed support for the use of these rules, the children were presented with problems in which the pre-transformation state contained two rows of four equally spaced counters. They first judged whether the numbers were the same and then had to repeat their judgement after a counter was added or subtracted or the rows were lengthened or shortened. Therefore in every case, Siegler's tasks amounted to a two-question format.

Even if the effects of repeated questioning did not exist, rule-complexity did not very strictly predict the children's performance. The 4-year-olds' responses on comparing small number sets were particularly puzzling. They solved less than half the problems in which there was a conflict between density and length but nothing was added or subtracted. As Siegler comments (1981, p. 54), the finding is not explainable in terms of counting, pairing, or "subitising" (estimating numbers perceptually without the use of a cognitive strategy). He ends up by offering the interpretation that children may believe a quantitative comparison is not necessary where a transformation without addition or subtraction takes place. This suggestion is in keeping with the observation that children have some understanding of abstract concepts; they can often measure and conserve but need to be shown when these skills are needed. At the same time, repeated questioning can contravene the quantity rule in conversation. In the absence of the salient cues of addition and subtraction, it may mislead children to change their initial responses.

The intriguing work of Flavell, Flavell, and Green (1983) follows in the tradition of the DeVries (1969) study on children's inability to distinguish perceptual appearance from reality. For Flavell and his colleagues, there are two types of conceptual difficulties in their understanding of the appearance–reality distinction. When asked to report reality, they instead report appearance. This difficulty is termed "phenomenism" and is said to be characteristic of non-conservation in young children. The converse is "realism" where they report reality when asked to report appearance.

In a series of three experiments, Flavell and his co-workers gave 3- and 4-year-olds problems in which they were asked to report, say, on the appearance and real composition of an object. For example, the children were shown an object that looked like an egg but was actually a stone painted white. They were then asked pairs of questions about the object while viewing it under three conditions: clear plastic (identity), dark plastic to make it look blue (colour), and a magnifier/minifier to make it appear to change in size. The questions were, "When you look at this with your eyes right now, does it look like a stone or does it look like an egg? What is this really, really? Is it really, really a stone or is it really, really an egg?" Many 3-year-olds did not make the distinction between appearance and reality. In the identity condition, they gave reality answers to both questions (realism) and in the colour and size conditions they gave appearance answers (phenomenism). Flavell et al. (1983, p. 117) interpreted the results to indicate a "general metacognitive limitation concerning mental representations". While young children use such representations, they are said to be less knowledgeable about their source and less aware of the origins of appearances. They do not easily process indirect or second-hand information.

Contrary to Piaget, the Flavell experiments have shown that pre-schoolers as young as 4-years-of-age often do have the capacity to distinguish perceptual appearance from reality. However, before focusing on conceptual difficulties, as limited as these may be, it is necessary to note that children might not share the experimenter's purpose in questioning or know when to apply an appropriate strategy. At the age of 3, they might distinguish between appearance and reality but they do not have the manner to convey this distinction. In the procedure used by Flavell, they may be trying to supply satisfactory, desirable "cute" answers to a continuous flow of questions on one topic that may be tacitly perceived as redundant or having obvious answers and so to contravene the quantity and relevance rules. In an effort to please, a child may be implicitly attributing to the experimenter the ability to change the properties of objects. He or she may then be excused.

Consider one further aspect of the experimental context: children have friendships and relations with other children and these may affect their

FIG. 2.4 A child giving an appearance answer when asked to report reality: an illustration of the possible context of "phenomenism" errors on an appearance–reality task which children perceive to be attractive.

responses. They may not indicate a deep, explicit knowledge of the distinction between appearance and reality (or knowledge on many other measures for that matter) owing either to the apprehension or attraction of communication with the grown-up (consistent with Explanations Two and Three discussed previously). The latter possibility is illustrated in Fig. 2.4. To be sure, there is a further very recent body of evidence that has been interpreted to support the claim of "conceptual difficulties" in 3-year-olds. This will be discussed in the section on "A 'theory of mind' in the child?" in Chapter Four.

The general difficulty is one of a lack of communication in natural language. On the basis of interviews or experiments that depart from conversational rules, we may wrongly conclude a limitation in understanding. Accordingly, it must be recognised that negative evidence on children's problem solving is almost inevitably vulnerable to weakness for they may simply have misunderstood the question or have interpreted the experimental context to require a particular answer. Positive results from experiments on children's knowledge are more informative for these show what children do, or what they are capable of doing, even though they may not have a full-blown understanding.

To establish children's knowledge of abstract concepts such as invariance in number is a matter that might be seen to require repeated or prolonged questioning or the use of certain forms of language. But through these sincere attempts to gain insight into processes of development, an experimenter may inadvertently neglect children's appreciation of the purpose and meaning of language and infer that they share the pragmatic force of an adult's questioning.

Children may be uncertain of the answer to the task in the first place and be induced to respond incorrectly, or they may be confident and know the answer but respond incorrectly because they read insincerity into the motives of the experimenter. Even if they do understand the experimenter's purpose, they may give incorrect answers to seek attention or to shorten or prolong the testing session. Then we have the problem that the experimenter's use of words may not yet map on to their experience. These are complex issues that can be approached by explicitly diagnosing the nature of the co-operation contained in the discourse of the experiment as well as that which is implicit in the task itself. Innovative methods of eliciting knowledge from children are required that are sensitive to their experience in communication and which avoid an excessive reliance on the sophisticated conversational implicatures used by adults.

Even infants have an appreciation of the identity of persons and objects. At an early age, they know that it is the same person or object that reappears despite perceptual changes. Because this "skeletal" knowledge constrains children to acquire theories about the mental and physical world, the architecture of children's minds does not rule out an implicit knowledge of abstract concepts such as invariance in number, though this understanding can be obscured in settings where well-meaning experimenters set aside conversational rules.

Therefore, children's interpretation of language in experiments cautions against the use of conservation as a building block to take leaps in theories of child development. A more solid foundation comes from their success on tasks where experimenters have not strayed from conversational rules.

3 Detecting Causality

CAUSALITY, CLASSIFICATION AND CONVERSATION

Piaget claimed that children's knowledge of cause and effect relations is limited to what they see. In *Judgement and Reasoning in the Child* (Piaget, 1928, p. 4), he characterised their ideas about causality to be restricted by "syncretism": "the spontaneous tendency . . . to take things in by means of a comprehensive act of perception instead of by the detection of details, to find immediately and without analysis analogies between words or objects that have nothing to do with each other, to bring heterogeneous phenomena into relation with each other, to find a reason for a chance event; in a word, it is the tendency to connect everything with everything else." If asked to complete the beginning of a sentence such as "The man fell off his bicycle because . . .", children under 5 or 6 years will respond "because he broke his arm" rather than, say, "because he lost his balance." On this basis, Piaget denied that young children can detect causal relations. He contended that their thinking is muddled and chaotic, and that their propositions about events are juxtaposed together instead of causally linked.

More detailed evidence came from tasks devised in Piaget's later work with Barbel Inhelder (Inhelder & Piaget, 1958). For example, an experimenter showed children an apparatus resembling a billiard game. Picture targets could be hit by using a rubber buffer to shoot a ball against a projection wall. The ball would rebound back to the interior of the apparatus where the targets were located. Inhelder and Piaget reported that children under about 7 to 8 years-of-age could not take note of the presence of angles at the rebound point and were unable to locate the operating mechanism. The equality of the angles of incidence and retraction was often discovered much later in adolescence.

Of course a distinction has to be made between children's capacity to identify causal relations and their explicit awareness that there is a useful relationship to be found that prevails over alternative magical or supernatural explanations. Inhelder and Piaget (1958, p. 4) remarked that young players on the billiard game apparatus are "most concerned with their practical success, without consideration of means; often even the role of rebounds is overlooked." It does not follow, however, that they are limited in their causal knowledge. Whether they play this type of game seriously in a manner that reflects their capacity for understanding causality is unclear.

Not only did Piaget judge young children to be incapable of identifying causal relations but he contended that they assign internal states and motives to inanimate objects. For example, in his early work, Piaget (1929) asked children questions such as "Can a bench feel anything if someone burnt it?" or "Are bicycles alive?" He interpreted their answers to indicate that young children's notions of causality are primitive and reflect an inability to distinguish between subjects and objects. They believe that any object may possess consciousness at a particular moment, especially a thing which moves like a bicycle.

Piaget also used children's responses in his clinical interviews to illustrate the primitive state of their ideas about causality. His approach is well represented by their explanations for the appearance of shadows and for the origin of dreams. For example, Piaget (1930, p. 184) reported an interview with a 5-year-old named "Stei" on the nature and cause of shadows:

Interviewer: *You know what a shadow is?*
Stei: *Yes, it's the trees that make them, under the tree.*
Interviewer: *Why is there a shadow under the tree?*
Stei: *Because there are a lot of leaves. The leaves make it.*
Interviewer: *How do they do it?*
Stei: *Because they are pink.*
Interviewer: *What does that do?*
Stei: *It makes a shadow.*
Interviewer: *Why?*
Stei: *Because inside [the leaves] it is night, inside.*
Interviewer: *Why?*
Stei: *Because it's day on top. The leaves are big and it is night inside them.* (Stei is shown his shadow on the ground)

Interviewer: *There is a shadow there?*
Stei: *Yes, the chair does it.*
Interviewer: *Why does the chair make a shadow?*
Stei: *Because it's black underneath. It's dark.*
Interviewer: *Why?*
Stei: *Why, because it is dark under the chair, because it's a chair and there is an edge and that keeps the shadow under the chair.*

For Piaget, young children typically believe that a shadow is a substance emanating from the object but participating with the night. They realistically attribute animistic qualities to leaves in projecting shadows. Only with increasing age do children know how shadows are projected and deny that objects cast shadows at night.

Similarly, Piaget proposed that young children misunderstand the nature of dreams; they believe that dreams originate from outside and remain external to the self. For example, Piaget (1929, p. 118) reports an interview with a 7-year-old named Mort:

Interviewer: (Where do you see dreams?)
Mort: *Against the wall.*
Interviewer: *Should I see them if I was there?*
Mort: *Yes.*
Interviewer: *Where do they come from?*
Mort: *From outside.*
Interviewer: *What sends them?*
Mort: *People.*
Interviewer: *What do you dream of?*
Mort: *A man being run over.*
Interviewer: *Is he in front of you when you dream, or inside you?*
Mort: *In front of me.*
Interviewer: *Where?*
Mort: *Under my window.*
Interviewer: *Should I have seen him if I had been there?*
Mort: *Yes.*
Interviewer: *Did you see him in the morning?*
Mort: *No.*
Interviewer: *Where did this dream come from? . . . Did you make it, or someone else?*
Mort: *Someone else.*
Interviewer: *Who?*
Mort: *A man my father knows (the one who was run over).*
Interviewer: *Does he make all the dreams?*
Mort: *Only that one.*
Interviewer: *And the others–*
Mort: *Other men.*

According to Piaget, older children believe that dreams originate and take place within the head. Even so, children under the age of 7 or 8 years may mistake the experimenter's purpose in asking questions about causal relations. Should they perceive the questions to contravene the conversational rules of relevance and quality (to be informative and sincere), they may offer silly or "cute" answers instead of the correct ones of which they are capable. Even so, interviewing that is liable to involve such questioning continues to be used as a sole or primary technique to obtain information about child development. An example that stands out comes from some of the very interesting work of Frank Keil. It provides one clear example of how modern developmental psychologists are often willing to venture that they have uncovered patterns of changes in children based on their responses in interview situations.

In his earlier studies, Keil (1979, pp. 109–110) reported children's answers to a sequence of interview questions. For example, in a manner reminiscent of Piaget, he provides an interchange between an experimenter and a child aged 4 years 2 months, on the nature of dreams:

E: *Can dreams be tall?*
C: *Yeah.*
E: *How tall?*
C: *Big, big, big* (spreads arms).
E: *Where are dreams?*
C: *In your bedroom.*
E: *In the daytime?*
C: *No, they're outside.*
E: *Could you see a dream?*
C: *Yeah.*
E: *How?*
C: *They're red.*
E: *What are they like?*
C: *They're made out of rock.*
E: *Could they be heavy?*
C: *Yeah, and they can't break either.*
E: *What do they look like?*
C: *They look like rocks. Like they're asleep on the grass. And the kids go outside and they see the things asleep.*
E: *Are dreams alive then?*
C: *No, they're not dead either. They just got grass on them.*

To demonstrate a systematic pattern of errors in children's early knowledge of "conceptual distinctions", Keil (1983) used this type of interview technique in a later series of three studies. Based on their responses, he maintained that young children are not easily able to distinguish between predicates (e.g., "happened yesterday") that apply to events and those that apply to physical objects (e.g., "shiny").

For example, in a first study, children in kindergarten and grades 2 and 4 were asked to judge 63 sentences as "OK" or "silly". These consisted of all combinations of three physical object terms (chair, rock, car) and three events (trip, party, storm) with nine predicates, some of which were applicable to physical objects and others to events. The test was to judge sentences like "The rock is heavy" as OK and those like "The car has ended" as silly. Kindergarten children were more likely than older ones to judge incorrectly the application of physical object predicates to events as acceptable (for example, "The storm is upside-down"). When this type of mistake occurred, it took the form of a consistent pattern across all combinations of physical object predicates and event terms. By contrast, a misapplication of event predicates to physical object terms occurred occasionally for some children. Keil's interpretation (1983, pp. 356–366) was "that there is a stage in concept differentiation in which the child knows very well what physical objects are but is confused about the nature of many events and about their distinguishing properties."

However, a closer look at this method of assessing children's knowledge of concepts suggests an alternative explanation. They were repeatedly questioned not only on the 63 sentences but on sentences involving polar opposites of the predicates. In each instance, an elaborate probe question procedure was used (see Fig. 3.1). The youngest children were seen individually, often in four half-hour sessions, and the occasional kindergarten child had to be dropped from the research because of a refusal to continue in all the sessions. Keil's rationale for the use of this technique was to ensure that responses were not influenced by fatigue or uncertainty. But alternatively, from the child's point of view, the experimenter's attempts to elicit "silly" judgements may have been perceived as a contravention of the quantity rule and interpreted as an invitation to give silly answers.

Given the type of interview questions, children may conclude that sentences like "The dream is tall" or "The storm is upside-down" are invariably cute and therefore consistently OK. By contrast, sentences containing combinations of physical object terms and event predicates such as "The rock has ended" hold no such attraction.

Keil's position is closely related to Piaget's (1970) hypothesis that young children have difficulty with tasks which require a knowledge of part–whole or "inclusion" relations. To illustrate, children may be shown bunches of flowers, many of them roses, and asked, "Are there more roses or more flowers?" Typically, they say that there are more roses.

Piagetians have taken children's responses on class inclusion problems to demonstrate that they are at a preoperational stage in their ability to

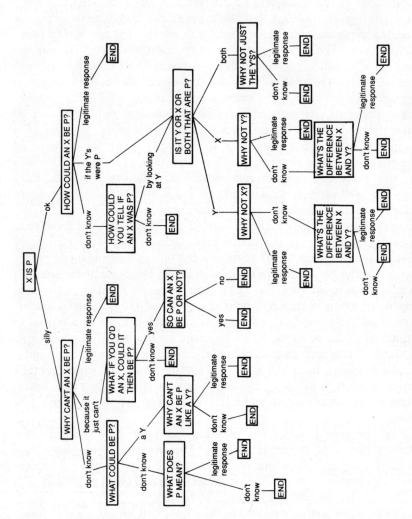

FIG. 3.1 Flowchart of the questioning procedure used by Keil (1979).

44

understand concepts. Since a knowledge of inclusion relations and how animate and inanimate objects ought to be included in classes is essential to detect causal events in nature, Keil's work might be regarded as evidence for a limitation in children's understanding of scientific concepts. At the same time, however, responses on inclusion problems demonstrate once more how children are sensitive to unconventional or unfamiliar forms of language that depart from conversational rules.

CHILDREN AS YOUNG SCIENTISTS

Recently, the early ability to understand causal relations and to distinguish between the properties of animate and inanimate objects has been intensively re-examined. The results challenge Piaget's assertion that young children lack causal knowledge as well as Keil's notion of a limitation in their ability to differentiate concepts.

One of the most intelligent studies of causality has been carried out by Shultz (1982b). To take Shultz's Experiment 3 as an example, children aged 3, 5, 7, and 9 years were given three problems. They saw: (1) an electric blower and a lamp directed toward a spot of light on the wall; (2) an electric blower and tuning fork directed toward a candle light which was then extinguished; and (3) a lamp and tuning fork directed toward the opening of a wooden box which began to resonate audibly.

Even many of the 3-year-olds were able to determine the cause of the effect. They told the experimenter that the lamp created the spot of light on the wall, the electric blower extinguished the candlelight, and the tuning fork made the sound come from the box. The children were able to identify the blower as irrelevant to the spot of light, the tuning fork as irrelevant to the candle, and the lamp as irrelevant to the sound from the box. Shultz concluded that young children can understand cause and effect relations in a sophisticated "generative" sense rather than as the simple covariation of two events at the same point in time. (For a further discussion, see Shultz, Fisher, Pratt, & Ruff, 1986.)

To determine whether young children can distinguish between the properties of animate and inanimate objects, Bullock (1985) gave 3- to 5-year-olds and adults four films depicting either an inanimate object (a multicoloured stack of wooden blocks or a plastic wind-up worm) or an animate object (a 2-year-old girl or a rabbit). The objects were first stationary on a flat surface and then moved until a bowl of crackers was reached. The children were asked questions about each object such as "Can (x) grow bigger? If we forget to give (x) food, will it get hungry? If (x) breaks, can we fix it with glue?" Most of the 4- and 5-year-olds performed like adults. While the 3-year-olds made a greater number of errors, the majority were still able to stipulate whether an object was alive or not.

Massey and Gelman (1988) have further established that 3- and 4-year-olds are able to use the distinction between animate and inanimate objects in deciding whether an object can move by itself. Children were given glossy photographs of unfamiliar mammals (e.g, a sloth, a pygmy marmoset), non-mammalian animals (e.g., a praying mantis, a freshwater crayfish), statues of animals (e.g., a figuring with insect-like eyes), wheeled vehicles (e.g., an electric golf caddy, an antique large-wheeled bicycle), and rigid objects consisting of more than one part (e.g., a robot). Instead of mistakenly using general or prototypical animal parts and shapes to guide their judgements of self-movement, the children were able to make correct inferences based on the visible movement-enabling features of each object. They were able to distinguish objects that can initiate their own movements from those for which movement must depend on an external source.

The results described by Bullock and by Massey and Gelman differ somewhat from those in other studies. Dolgin and Behrend (1984) found that a large minority of 5-year-olds (45%) attribute animate properties to dolls, and Carey (1985b, p. 91) reported that many of the 4-year-olds in her study believe a mechanical monkey eats (40%), sleeps (30%), and has bones (30%). But since children are liable to perceive violations of conversational rules in questioning about their causal knowledge, at least some may have misunderstood the experimenter's purpose and have given pretend answers instead of correct ones. For instance, the genuine belief of some children may have been that dolls and mechanical monkeys are inanimate objects just as a stone, a vehicle, or a garlic press. The possibility remains to be tested, for example, in studies where children are asked to give attributions for the correct and incorrect choices of peers.

Might a similar concern lead to reservations about Keil's evidence which suggests that young children have difficulties in inclusion relations? Carol Smith (1979) approached this issue by examining the effects of presentation order on their responses. In a series of experiments 4- to 6-year-olds were asked questions on the inclusion of persons and objects into classes. Some of these referred to items where X was a subset of Y (e.g., "Are all boys people?"); others concerned items where X was a superset of Y (e.g., "Are all animals cats?"). Similar to Keil's material that required a "silly" answer, the X and Y items were disjointed in a third set of questions (e.g., "Are all spoons bumblebees?").

Smith took care to ensure that the children included in her studies understood the words "all" and "some". In paying special attention to the effects of prolonged questioning on the 18 "quantified inclusion" questions given to the children in her first study, she discovered significant differences between performance on the first half of the questions and the second. On the first half, most of the children answered correctly. Performance on the second half fell off sharply, particularly for the younger children. However, contrary to the hypotheseis that young children have a general conceptual limitation as shown by a consistent difficulty with all the class inclusion problems, errors were usually on only one type of item. In her follow-up studies, Smith reduced the number of questions and found that even 4-year-olds performed significantly better than would be predicted by chance.

As shown by the pattern of responses on Smith's measures, the basic format of children's representation of concepts may be the same as in older children and adults. Their difficulties may be in drawing out the consequences of this representation or in misinterpreting the force of the experimenter's intent. As Smith (1979, p. 454) remarks, children who made mistakes were frequently answering the wrong question (for example, Experimenter's question: "Are all animals dogs?" Child's response: "Yes, 'cause I know what dogs are." Experimenter's question: "Are all robins birds?" Child's response: "No, 'cause there are other kinds of birds.")

For children to express an explicit knowledge of inclusion relations in interviews with adults requires extensive conversational experience. A team of psychologists working in Scotland (McGarrigle, Grieve, & Hughes, 1978) has shown that 4- to 6-year-olds have much difficulty when comparing one row of four cows (two black and two white) with a second row of four horses (three black and one white). When asked to say whether there were more black horses or more cows, only 5 of 48 children gave the correct answer that there were more cows. However, as the Scottish psychologists point out, the children's responses do not necessarily point to a lack of knowledge about classes. Their presuppositions of what the task requires them to do are tied to the salient features of their environment (in this case, colour). They have little experience of the formal usage of language used by adult questioners that is founded on the implicit message, "Ignore the colours that you see. Just think about the logic of my question." To novices on inclusion problems, colour may seem the most reasonable way to compare quantities. After all, they could well reason, why would an adult show a child objects of different colours if colour was not a good way to compare quantities?

In this way, as may often be the case in experiments, many questions which require children to make judgements about causality and classification can inadvertently violate the rule of ordinary conversation that a speaker's messages should be relevant. If listeners are inexperienced in the world of adult conversation, they may strive to grant relevance to an otherwise senseless question and respond as if the speaker really meant that the properties of the objects to be compared are relevant to the correct answer. It cannot be assumed that children share the experimenter's definition of the attributes relevant to the task.

In view of the research that points to preschoolers' ability to distinguish between the properties of animate and inanimate objects, a conversational reinterpretation of Keil's results is a distinct possibility. But at the least, although there remain several grounds to challenge Keil's analysis of conceptual development (see Carey, 1985b), he has drawn attention to the importance of studying children's knowledge of ontology or basic categories of existence. In at least some cases, children can be capable young scientists in detecting causal relations and classifying objects and events.

JUDGEMENTS OF TIME

According to the "principle of priority", causes must precede their effects. Since to understand causality it is necessary to be conscious of how sequences of events lead to psychological states, children's early grasp of causal relations presupposes a knowledge of the priority principle. This knowledge is shown in their awareness of random and deliberate phenomena, their understanding of the words used to describe time, and their estimation of distance and duration.

The research of Kuzmak and Gelman (1986) suggests that children can distinguish between random and deliberate events. In their study, 3- to 7-year-olds were shown two physical phenomena: a marble cage game in which marbles would trickle out haphazardly at random, and a marble tube game in which a marble at the end of the tube would roll out if released by a knob. For each problem, the children were asked: "When you play with this game here, do you know which colour is going to come out? Yes or no?"

Correct responses were given by children aged 4 and older. While the 3-year-olds did not differentiate between the random and determinate phenomena, they did not treat either event as predictable. As Kuzmak and Gelman suggest, the youngest children may have just misunderstood the question. Similarly, in two experiments, Sophian and Huber (1984) found that 5-year-olds showed an appreciation of the priority principle while the performance of 3-year-olds was at a chance level. However, the younger children experienced prolonged testing. In fact, in Sophian and Huber's first experiment, they were asked to make 64 judgements. Under these conditions, the children may not have revealed their understanding of causality.

Whatever the interpretation of experiments on knowledge of the priority principle, by the age of 5 years, children have a grasp of words used to describe time such as "yesterday" and "tomorrow" and "always", "never", and "sometimes". For example, in a study by Harner (1975), children aged 2, 3, and 4 years were seen on two successive days. On the first day, they played with a set of toys and saw a bag with toys for the next day. On the second day, the children saw three sets of toys: those from yesterday, those for tomorrow, and "today's toys". The experimenter's requests were, "Show me a toy from yesterday" and "Show me a toy for tomorrow." The 2-year-olds did not comprehend differences in the three groups of toys. The 3-year-olds appeared to understand that "yesterday" did not refer to today's toys, and "yesterday" was better understood than "tomorrow". By the age of 4 years, "yesterday" and "tomorrow" were understood equally well.

In a similar series of experiments on the acquisition of words such as "never", Kuczaj (1975) gave preschoolers (mean age, 4 years) pairs of sentences such as "The boy always drives the car. The girl never drives the car." The children were then asked, "Who drives the car?" In response to this procedure, most children treated "never" as a negative. Words such as "always" and "sometimes" were often correctly regarded as a positive.

In keeping with children's knowledge of causality and their compre-hension of time words, several experiments have now demonstrated the early ability to make accurate judgements of duration. Levin (1982) reported a series of experiments in which preschoolers were able to infer relative durations from differences in starting and ending points. For example, children were shown two lights and were asked to judge whether the lights were lit for the same time, and if not which light was on for the longer time. The majority of preschoolers could respond correctly, although performance declined when the lights were presented with inter-fering cues such as differential brightness and size. These results under-mine Piaget's claims that young children judge time simply by taking account of either starting or ending points and that they lack the ability to integrate the two points together.

Wilkening (1981) presented three age groups (5–6 years, 9–10 years, and adults) with a set of three tasks to examine the abilities to integrate information about velocity and time, velocity and distance, and distance and time. For example, in the task on velocity and time integration, a frightful-looking toy dog was made to bark for 2, 5, or 8 seconds. The children and adults were required to estimate the distance travelled by a turtle, guinea pig, and cat during each time interval by placing pictures of the animals along a miniature drawbridge. In sharp contrast to Piaget, all age groups were able to integrate velocity and time according to the multiplying model: judged distance = time × velocity. The greater the time and the quicker the velocity of the animal, the longer the estimated distance.

On the two other tasks, there were clear developmental differences. Compared to the 9- and 10-year-olds and adults, the 5- and 6-year-olds were less able to judge time on the basis of the distance travelled by the three animals, or to differentiate which of seven animals (a snail, turtle, guinea pig, mouse, cat, deer, and horse) could cover various distances (70, 140, and 210cm) in relation to different time intervals. However, in the former task, time information was not "visually present". The children could only respond by pressing a key to let a toy dog bark for a certain time. An overload on the child's memory may have prevented the use of a sophisticated multiplication strategy. The memory demands of the latter task were also high; the children were required to judge the comparative speeds of seven different animals for each of three distances.

More recent studies have established that young children are able to distinguish the durations of everyday activities. For example, Wilkening, Levin, and Druyan (1987) found that, by the age of 6 years, children can use counting as a strategy to estimate time in successive events. Friedman (1988) gave 3- to 9-year-olds a task in which they could point to sandglasses of different sizes in order to represent the duration of five events depicted on cards: drinking milk, shopping, a family car trip, one cartoon show, and sleeping at night. While performance improved between 3 and 6 years, even 3-year-olds estimated true normative durations at an above chance level.

Reliable evaluations of others' actions on accurate estimates of time intervals. As Wilkening (1982, p. 110) has astutely observed: "From the point of view of an applied developmental psychology, for example, it is of interest to know under what conditions children can integrate time, distance, and velocity in everyday life decisions . . . how children combine two or more velocities of objects moving at different directions at different distances, when estimating time of collision or safe passing." These judgements require perceptual estimations as well as knowledge about time, velocity, and distance.

While in everyday situations children may accord less recognition to the constraints of time, it is also noteworthy that adults themselves often bend time to suit the circumstances. Perhaps the most vivid illustrations of real-life distortions of time can be found in literature. In many novels, time has been stretched or condensed. This feature is not limited to the works of Joyce and Proust. Borges (1964) in his story *The Secret Miracle* graphically depicts how a second could be stretched into a year through the will of a condemned man facing execution in Czechoslovakia during the Second World War.

EXPERIMENTS ON CHILDREN'S KNOWLEDGE OF HEALTH AND ILLNESS

Although children do better on causal tasks with increasing age, they show more than a limited capacity to understand causality. They often succeed at a level that exceeds what would be expected by chance alone. Many of their shortcomings may also have less to do with a limitation on their ability to understand causal relations then with the language used in experiments. When questions have been devised to avoid redundancy and to promote relevance, the research often contradicts Piaget's original position with implications that are applied as well as theoretical.

A key applied issue concerns the nature of children's conceptions of health and illness (for reviews, see Burbach & Peterson, 1986; Eiser, 1985; Maddux, Roberts, Sledden, & Wright, 1986). On the one hand, should it be accepted that young children generally mistake appearances for reality and that they are unable to detect cause and effect, there would be little point in informing them about health-related matters. On the other hand, evidence that young children have an understanding of the nature of illness would have significance for education and preventive health.

Bibace and Walsh (1981) proposed a Piagetian stage analysis of children's knowledge of the causes of illness. Children between 2 and 6 years of age account for illness by immediate temporal or physical cues. People are said to catch colds from magic, or from the sun, trees, or God. Later children say that colds are caught when someone else goes near them and when touched by sick persons. Finally, at approximately 11-years-of-age, they give "formal–logical" explanations. There is a differentiation between external and internal causal agents. While a cold may be transmitted by an external agent, the illness is located within the body. Children may describe colds as transmitted by viruses and consisting of blockages in the sinuses and lungs.

In fact, according to Bibace and Walsh, young children may regard all illness as contagious and believe that toothaches, as well as colds, can be caught by proximity to a sick person. Since children cannot reason about causality, they may view illness as punishment. Bibace and Walsh go on to suggest that the clinical usefulness of a Piagetian theory for the prevention and treatment of illness in children is to promote empathy with the irrational childish fears of the young and to communicate children's immature understanding to health professionals. For example, health workers should be told that closeness to a sick person may be unnerving and, because children have only a limited appreciation of the nature of contagion, they may request to be moved away lest they catch the illness themselves.

Guided by this type of Piagetian account, Kister and Patterson (1980) investigated children's understanding of contagion and their belief in punishment or "immanent justice" explanations for illness. The subjects were 15 healthy children in each of 4 groups: preschool, kindergarten, second grade, and fourth grade. The interviewer used a cold as an example of a common contagious illness, a toothache as an example of a common non-contagious illness, and a scraped knee as an example of a common accident. In each instance, the children were given questions such as "If a boy (or girl) your age went to school one day, and the girl sitting next to him had a cold (or two other ailments), would he have to be careful so he wouldn't catch the cold from her? Why (not)? Can the boy catch the cold? [If the child answered in the affirmative, the following questions were asked.] Let's say the boy really didn't want to get the cold. Would it be better for him to sit next to the girl with the cold, across the room from her, or does it make a difference where he sits? Why (not)?"

The children then received questions to determine whether they interpret illness to be punishment for naughtiness. The interviewer said, "Once a boy your age disobeyed his mother. Was that a nice thing to do? Well, that afternoon, he got a cold (or other ailment). Do you think he got a cold because he disobeyed his mother? What made him get a cold? Let's pretend he didn't disobey his mother. Do you think he would get a cold anyway? Why (not)?.

Using this method, the children in preschool (mean age = 4 years, 8 months) and kindergarten (mean age = 5 years 6 months) appeared to generalise contagion to ailments such as a toothache and scraped knee. They did not seem to understand the role of distance in the transmission of contagious illnesses. In stark opposition to the work of Shultz and others, Kister and Patterson concluded that young children are biased to regard all contiguous events as causally related. Even on a control story in which the boy who had helped his mother later lost some money, 11 of the 15 preschoolers affirmed a causal relationship when asked questions such as, "Did he lose the money because he helped his mother?" Most importantly, children who offered incorrect responses were very likely to give punishment explanations for the causes of illness.

In addition, Rozin, Fallon, and Augustoni-Ziskind (1985; see also Rozin & Fallon, 1987, pp. 34–35) have claimed that young children do not easily understand the invisible nature of contamination. In their study, an experimenter dropped substances such as a used comb and a grasshopper into glasses of juice. In line with the results of an earlier interview (Fallon, Rozin, & Pliner, 1984), a considerable number of 4- to 6-year-olds drank the juice on request.

On this basis, it has been concluded that young children do not understand contagion and contamination as causes of illness. Instead they may express a belief in immanent justice. However, as Rozin et al. (1985) have cautioned, the effect of social pressure on responses is difficult to evaluate. In this respect, the evidence has often come from studies in which children have been subjected to forms of prolonged or unconventional questioning that may be perceived to depart from the conversational rule to be sincere.

Under this procedure, children's inconsistent responses again may not reflect the depth of their understanding. Rather than lacking knowledge of the causes of illness, they may simply have misinterpreted what they were required to do. For example, children may know that a drink which has been in contact with a foreign object can be harmful and they may reject the object as food. At the same time, they may not be aware that a grown-up might offer children a contaminated drink and insincerely imply—in violation of the quality rule—that the drink is safe in a well-meaning effort to test their understanding. In studies to ascertain whether they believe that illness is punishment, they may attempt to comply with the suggestion of an adult interviewer: adults are so powerful that children who are naughty will inevitably be punished. For these reasons, it is premature to conclude that young children do not have the ability to distinguish between contagious and non-contagious ailments, to understand the nature of contamination, and to discount immanent justice as an explanation for illness.

Even if some children do have a genuine belief in immanent justice and illness as punishment, there is another objection to the form of Piagetian analysis which has been adopted by researchers such as Kister and Patterson: immanent justice is by no means a mode of explanation limited to children. Shweder (1977; 1986), an anthropologist, stresses forcefully that many adults as well as children believe in magical or unnatural explanations for events and that these beliefs are rational in a world where resemblance is not a good predictor of the likelihood that an event will occur or coincide with another. He provides a rather macabre anecdote to illustrate the extent to which children have unnatural explanations for cause and effect relations (Shweder, 1977, p. 637). This is not for the squeamish: "A little boy . . . tried to prove that spiders hear with their legs. After cutting of spider's legs, he yelled, "Jump" The spider did not jump. So the little boy said, "You see, I was right. Spiders hear with their legs."

During the 19th century, adults often professed similar, primitive views about the nature of illness that were tied to visible events. They believed that cholera epidemics in the United States were due to punishment for leading an immoral lifestyle, and such beliefs are present today among many adults in both industrial and non-industrial societies as explanations for the spread of venereal disease and AIDS (Brandt, 1987; Murdock, 1980; Rosenberg, 1962). Both children and adults may be prone to immanent justice explanations in an environment where alternatives are not available or are unappealing, and researchers may seriously entertain the proposal that, to some extent, magical thinking is universally present in normal adults.

UNDERSTANDING CONTAGION AND CONTAMINATION

I sought to re-examine children's knowledge of contagion and contamination in a series of three experiments (Siegal, 1988a). Since direct, prolonged questioning on notions about health and illness may result in a contravention of the quantity and quality rules and a misinterpretation of the task requirements, the children were asked to evaluate others' explanations for illness, to indicate the likelihood that illness would occur, and to predict their own preventive health behaviour. Different children were included in each experiment.

In Experiment One, children considered immanent justice, contagion, and contamination as causes of illness. I hypothesised that they would be able to differentiate accurately between contagious and immanent justice explanations for contagious and non-contagious ailments and to identify foreign substances as sources of contamination. The 120 participants were divided into three groups of 40. The mean ages in years and months with ranges in parentheses were preschool, 4-11 (4-6 to 5-4), Grade 1, 5-9 (5-5 to 6-2), and Grade 3, 8-3 (7-6 to 8-7).

The experiment consisted of two phases. Half the children received one phase first, and half the other phase first. In the first phase on contagion, the experimenter showed each child four videotaped segments of puppets in a random order. Each segment was approximately 60 seconds long. In two of the segments, the puppets were shown to be suffering from a cold. In the other two, they were shown to be suffering from a toothache. In one instance for each of the ailments, the puppets told an adult female questioner on the videotape (who was not the same person as the experimenter) that they caught the ailment when playing with a friend; in the other, the puppets claimed that they caught the ailment through naughty behaviour that included playing with a forbidden pair of scissors. After each segment, the children were asked two questions: (1) "Is the puppet right or wrong?" (2) For the segments on immanent justice, "Can children get (the ailment) by being naughty?" For the segments on proximity, "Can children get (the ailment) by playing with a friend who had (the ailment)?"

In the second phase on contamination, the children were given three situations in a random order. An insect, comb, and spoon were shown to fall accidently to the bottom of a glass of milk just as a child (the same age and gender as the subject) was about to drink. The situations were illustrated with a real dead cockroach, comb, and spoon. The spoon did not look dirty but its actual cleanliness was not specified. The comb was obviously used with dandruff clearly stuck to it. The cockroach was obviously authentic and could be readily identified by all the children; it was used since pilot work suggested that contact with insects such as flies and grasshoppers may not be sufficient to affect Australian adults' judgements about contamination.

The experimenter asked the questions before and after she removed the object from the milk and placed it out of sight. The questions before removal of the object were: "Would the child get sick if she (or he) drank some of the milk with an (x) in it?" If yes, "A little or a lot?" The next question was, "Would you want to drink milk that had an (x) in it if a grown-up told you that you could?" The questions after the object was removed were: "Would the child get sick if she drank some of the milk now that the (x) had been taken out?" If yes, "A little or a lot?" Next question: "Would you want to drink milk that had an (x) taken out of it if a grown-up told you that you could?"

The responses in the contagion phase of Experiment One are shown in Table 3.1. The children often accepted the explanation that colds can be transmitted by proximity and rejected an immanent justice explanation. For all groups, correct answers for both types of explanations for colds were above a chance level. In the case of toothaches, the responses of the preschoolers and first graders did not exceed chance. In these two age groups, the knowledge that toothaches are not transmitted through proximity was correlated significantly with their rejection of immanent justice as a causal factor. As Kister and Patterson (1980) observed, a belief in immanent justice explanations may be associated with the absence of knowledge about contagion.

TABLE 3.1

Numbers of Children Out of 40 Responding Correctly in the Contagion Phase of Experiment One on Conceptions of the Causes of Illness (From Siegal, 1988a)

	Ailment			
	Cold		Toothache	
Group	Proximity	Immanent Justice	Proximity	Immanent Justice
Preschoolers				
Puppet right or wrong?	33 (83)	29 (73)	22 (55)	23 (58)
Can children catch it that way?	37 (93)	29 (73)	21 (53)	25 (63)
Grade 1				
Puppet right or wrong?	33 (83)	29 (73)	23 (58)	24 (60)
Can children catch it that way?	38 (95)	30 (75)	23 (58)	21 (53)
Grade 3				
Puppet right or wrong?	40 (100)	38 (95)	37 (93)	37 (93)
Can children catch it that way?	38 (95)	36 (90)	38 (95)	38 (95)

Note: Percentages are in parentheses rounded to the nearest whole number.

The children demonstrated expertise in the contamination phase study (see Table 3.2): 39 out of 40 preschoolers said that they would not drink milk with a cockroach inside and 34 said they would not drink even when the cockroach was removed. Most children claimed that to drink milk with a dirty comb inside or removed would make the child either a little or a lot sick. The majority would not drink the milk themselves in either of these two circumstances. It seemed, although further study is needed to investigate this possibility, that some of the few children who said that they would drink the milk which had been in contact with a cockroach or dirty comb intended to shock the experimenter. Surprisingly, 13 out of 40 preschoolers claimed that a child who drank milk with the spoon inside would become very sick. Many of these spontaneously volunteered that they would be afraid of swallowing the spoon! With the spoon removed, the number decreased to five.

Altogether, the children in our sample had a substantial knowledge of contagion and contamination as causes of illness. I carried out two additional experiments to determine whether they can distinguish between explanations for contagious ailments and accidents and to re-examine responses to milk in contact with a spoon. According to Kister and Patterson (1980), if physical contact is salient, young children are likely to infer a causal relationship between any two contiguous events and may fail to distinguish between contagious and non-contagious ailments and those

TABLE 3.2
Responses of the Children (Out of 40) in the Contamination Phase of Experiment One on Conceptions of the Causes of Illness (From Siegal, 1988a)

	Cockroach		Comb		Spoon	
	In	Out	In	Out	In	Out
Preschoolers						
Not sick	4	7	12	17	20	29
A little sick	2	5	9	7	7	6
A lot sick	34	28	19	16	13	5
Not drink yourself	39	34	33	24	27	15
Grade 1						
Not sick	0	1	6	15	30	32
A little sick	6	12	18	14	6	7
A lot sick	34	24	16	11	4	1
Not drink yourself	39	37	37	32	20	8
Grade 3						
Not sick	1	2	6	7	39	39
A little sick	13	18	22	27	1	1
A lot sick	26	20	12	6	0	0
Not drink yourself	39	38	37	33	6	1

caused by accidents. Therefore, in a second experiment, preschoolers were asked to evaluate a child's explanation for a scraped knee and for contiguous events that could not have been causally related.

The participants in Experiment Two were 12 boys and 12 girls with a mean age of 4 years 11 months (range, 4-6 to 5-6). They were presented, in a randomised order with three stories about a child who had a scraped knee. In one story, the central figure incorrectly gave a contagious response and in a second, a correct non-contagious response. The third story acted as a control; it was used to test Kister and Patterson's assertion that young children infer causality in events that covary. The experimenter told the children, "Here are stories about some other children. I want you to tell me whether they were pretending or giving the right answer." The actual gender of the story characters was the same as the boys and girls questioned. For half the children, the order of the premises was reversed (Was he just pretending or could this be the right answer?). The male versions of the stories were:

1. A boy named Fred who was about your age had a scraped knee. A grown-up asked Fred how he got his scraped knee. Fred said he got it from sitting next to another boy with a scraped knee. Could this be the right answer or was he just pretending? (Contagious response—pretending.)
2. A boy named Bill who was about your age had a scraped knee. A grown-up asked Bill how he got his scraped knee. Bill said he got it from falling off a swing on to a sharp rock. Could this be the right answer or was he just pretending? (Non-contagious response—right answer.)
3. A boy named John who was about your age had a shirt with spots of wet purple paint. A grown-up asked John how he got spots of paint on his shirt. John said he got it from falling off a swing on to a sharp rock. Could this be the right answer or was he just pretending? (Control story.)

Of the 24 children, 22 judged correctly that the child who claimed he received the scraped knee through sitting next to another child with a scraped knee was pretending; and 19 felt that the child who said the scraped knee was caused by falling off a swing on a sharp rock could have been telling the right answer. Of the five other children who claimed that the child was pretending, only one was incorrect on either of the two other stories. Almost all of the children (22/24) attributed pretending to a child who claimed that the wet paint was due to falling on a sharp rock.

These responses were all above a chance level. At least in the case of a scraped knee, children do not ordinarily generalise their concept of contagion to include accidents. Contact alone does not guarantee an explanation involving contagion. Further, similar to Shultz's (1982b) results, young children do not regard a temporal concurrence of events to necessitate causation.

Experiment Three examined preschoolers' understanding of contamination in the spoon and milk situation of the first experiment. I expected that, if the cleanliness of the spoon was clarified, they would be likely to indicate that there would be no ill health effects from drinking the milk. The participants were 10 boys and 10 girls with a mean age of 4 years, 10 months (range = 4-6 to 5-6). They saw an experimenter wash a spoon and then say, "This is a very clean spoon. It has just been washed in hot water with soap suds, rinsed with clean water, and dried. Suppose that the spoon fell in the milk that a little boy (or girl) about your age was about to drink." The remainder of the procedure was similar to the contamination phase of Experiment One. The children were asked questions before and after the spoon was said to have been removed by a grown-up. The questions before were "Would the child get sick if he (or she) drank some of the milk which had a spoon in it being careful not to drink the spoon? A little or a lot? Would you want to drink milk that had a spoon in it if a grown-up told you that you could?" Then the children were told, "Suppose the spoon were taken out. Would the child get sick if he drank some of the milk now that the spoon had been taken out? A little or a lot? Would you want to drink milk that had a spoon taken out of it if a grown-up told you that you could?"

With the spoon inside, 17 of the 20 children indicated that the child would not get sick by drinking the milk, 3 said that the child would be a little sick, and only 5 said that they would not drink the milk themselves. With the spoon removed, the comparable numbers were 18, 2, and 5. These results were clearly superior to those in Experiment One, although responses were not unanimous. A small number of children may have been overly careful, and it remains to be determined whether some may have been mindful of possible allergies or reactions to milk.

The results of the three experiments are limited to a knowledge of contagion and contamination as causes of illness. Some ailments such as toothaches may have an internal or maturational basis, and research is required to probe children's understanding of internal body functions and their consequences (Eiser, 1985). Further, although the children in the studies often responded correctly, a minority did not; individual differences in knowledge about health-related matters merit additional attention.

Bearing these considerations in mind, children's knowledge of contagion and contamination has been underestimated in previous studies. Contrary to Bibace and Walsh (1981) and Kister and Patterson (1980), many preschoolers can identify contagion and dismiss immanent justice as an explanation for colds. They can understand that a scraped knee is a non-contagious ailment. At least in Western societies, immanent justice may be a factor in explanations for ailments such as toothaches only if the illness is not easily within personal experience and another explanation is not salient.

The possibility is left open that even younger children would have some capacity to display a knowledge of the consequences of ingesting contaminants. In one further experiment (Siegal & Share, 1990, Experiment One), we sought to test the hypothesis that 3-year-olds are sensitive to the invisible nature of contamination in a naturally occurring context and, accordingly, can make evaluations and inferences for others' false responses and choices about contamination. The participants were 48 children with a mean age of 43 months and range of 36 to 47 months. The experimenter spent about a week in the children's day care centres prior to testing in order to become acquainted with them. The experiment consisted of three phases in which the children were seen individually. Within each phase, the orders of the stories, questions and alternatives were counterbalanced. The actual names of the story characters were the same sex as the children.

In the first phase on contamination labelling, the experimenter told the children in the course of natural conversation during their snack time, "Here's some juice. Oh! It has a cockroach in it." The cockroach (*Periplaneta americana*) floated to the top. The experimenter removed it from sight without a trace and asked, "Is the juice OK or not OK to drink?"

In the second phase, the experimenter gave the children two stories and asked them to evaluate the responses of others. Story A was: "A grown-up poured juice into a glass with a cockroach in it. The cockroach floated on top and then the grown-up threw it away. He asked John, a boy your age, whether the juice would be OK to drink or whether it would make him sick? John said that the juice would be OK to drink. Was John right? Would it make him sick?" Responses to the last question were used as the evaluation measure. Story B was the same except that a child said the juice would make him sick.

In the third phase on inferences for others' false choices, the children were shown two glasses and told, "Here is some chocolate milk and here is some water. A cockroach fell into the chocolate milk. It floated on top. A grown-up pulled it out and threw it away. A boy named Jim came along to ask for a glass of chocolate milk which was his favourite drink. Jim didn't know the cockroach had fallen in. Which glass did Jim want? Which glass should the grown-up give him?" The experimenter displayed two signs and continued, "Jim wanted to tell other children that one of the two drinks would make them sick. He had two signs: 'happy face' and 'sad face'.

Which one should he choose to tell the children? You take the 'sad face' and put in front of that drink to tell them not to drink it." To establish the stability of contamination labelling, about two weeks later, a different experimenter who was unaware of the initial responses re-enacted the first phase using a different drink.

Table 3.3 shows that performance in all phases was above a chance level. Contrary to the notion that young children lack the capacity to comprehend the nature of contamination, 77% consistently responded that the juice was not good, 83% correctly evaluated the responses of other children to the incident in both stories, 67% correctly inferred that, while a child may want a chocolate drink, he or she should be given an alternative, and 75% chose a sad face without prompting as a warning against the drink. In all phases, the ages of the children were not correlated with the responses.

Although Rozin, Fallon, and Augustoni-Ziskind (1985) have maintained that young children do not readily understand the invisible nature of contamination, most preschoolers were unwilling to pronounce an apparently safe glass of milk as harmless after a foreign substance had been removed. Part of this discrepancy may be due to the different methods and foreign substances employed by Rozin and his colleagues in their American studies and to the comparatively ubiquitous nature of insects, and especially cockroaches, in the Australian environment. However, the results from these studies of Australian children are consistent with evi-

TABLE 3.3
Percentages of Children Responding Correctly in the Experiment on Contamination
Sensitivity in 3-year-olds (From Siegal & Share, 1990, Experiment One.)
Numbers (Out of 48) are in Parentheses

Labelling	
Responding on the first test that the juice is not good to drink despite appearance (removal of cockroach)	85 (41)
Responding on the second test that the juice is not good to drink despite appearance	85 (41)
Consistent on both tests	83 (40)
Consistent in indicating that the juice is not good	77 (37)
Evaluations	
"No" to a child's response: (A) the juice is OK	88 (42)
"Yes" to response: (B) the juice would cause sickness	90 (43)
"No" to response A "yes" to B	83 (40)
Inferences	
Child wants chocolate drink	77 (37)
Child should be given another drink	83 (40)
Responding both that a child wants a chocolate drink but should be given an alternative drink	67 (32)
Choosing "sad face" without prompting and correct use of sign to warn others	75 (36)

dence from other American studies that, by the age of 4, children can often distinguish between the real properties of objects and their outward appearances and can ignore perceptual appearances in classifying persons and objects on attributes such as blood type (S. Gelman, Collman, & Maccoby, 1986; see the section on gender concepts in Chapter Five).

Since to obtain nutrients is an activity that is prerequisite for fitness and survival, possibly very early in human development, children are constrained towards learning about contamination. They possess an implicit knowledge that can be drawn out with preventive health instruction from parents and caregivers. Of course children cannot be credited with a full-blown understanding. The research does not show that their sensitivity to contamination forms the basis for an early microscopic theory of illness. My proposal is only that they are constrained towards acquiring contamination sensitivity in the first place. This perspective is compatible with the position that young children are equipped with a skeletal implicit knowledge of abstract concepts such as causality. This knowledge may be brought to the surface should experimenters attend to using child-friendly techniques that consist of question that abide by the rules of conversation and convey elements of sincerity, non-redundancy, relevance, and clarity.

Young children's understanding of contagion and contamination has implications for education but not necessarily in the manner envisaged by the followers of Piaget. Bibace and Walsh (1981) claimed that instruction about health should be matched to children's stage of development because they do not have the cognitive prerequisites to benefit from causal knowledge. Our studies contradict this account and suggest that knowledge of the causes of illness is within the grasp of young children. Moreover, even preschoolers have an implicit theory of child care and advocate reasoning as a form of intervention against physical harm (see Chapter Six). Therefore, they should be receptive to methods of verbal instruction, possibly through the use of picture books that graphically illustrate the causes of illness (Berger, 1985).

Rather than maintaining that instruction about health and illness is most likely to be successful where information is "matched" to the particular concerns shown by children in a Piagetian stage when they do not understand causality, children's early causal knowledge may be used as a basis for preventive health education. Adults' appreciation of what children can or do know about contagion and contamination should promote communication with children on health matters. My hope is that this possibility will draw recognition to an area which cries out for attention. As Kleinman (1986, p. 226) has pointed out, psychology and related disciplines have been neglected in primary medical care despite the "epidemiological reality" that over 50% of clinical practice deals with the psychological and social aspects of illness. Here is a solid application of developmental psychology to health education and prevention.

4 Representing Objects and Viewpoints

SEEING AND KNOWING

Piaget used the term "egocentrism" more widely than to describe the ability of children who do not conserve. His claim was that egocentrism permeates young children's thinking and is a severe, general limitation on their knowledge of the world. He contended that they rely purely on the perceptual point of view when judging the visual perspectives of others and that they are not capable of understanding how another's viewpoint differs from their own. Their understanding of the physical world is "at first completely egocentric" (Piaget & Inhelder, 1956, p. 209), and it is the same egocentric orientation that prevents them from understanding others' perspectives, interests, intentions, and feelings.

A great variety of tasks have been used to measure the ability to take the perspective of others. Children have been shown displays of pictures, toys or blocks and asked to match photographs to the perspectives of different observers around a table. They have also been required to report on the percepts of an observer wearing sunglasses tinted a different colour than those worn by the children themselves (for reviews of these tasks, see Ford (1979; 1985) and Waters and Tinsley (1985)). However, the most prominent of all perspective-taking measures has been the "three-mountains" task.

In the description supplied by Piaget and Inhelder (1956, pp. 210–211), this task consists of a pasteboard model, 1 metre square at the base and from 12–30cm high (see Fig. 4.1). When seated in front of the model at the initial position (A), children view a small green mountain with a little house at the summit, a higher brown mountain topped with a red cross slightly to the rear of the green one, and the highest mountain which is grey with a snow peak. By pointing to photographs, for example, they can indicate what an observer views from different perspectives on the model (B, C, and D). Piaget and Inhelder (1956, p. 213) proposed that, on this type of task, children under 7 years are confined to reproducing their own point of view, "When a number of objects are involved, as in the case of the group of mountains, it is found that the child fails to realise that different observers will enjoy different perspectives and seems to regard his own point of view as the only one."

In a more recent test of children's perspective-taking, Liben (1978) asked 3- and 4-year-olds to report on percepts of coloured blocks as seen by the self and an experimenter. Rather than rotating a turntable to represent the display, they were required to point to a card that "shows the way the blocks look". The children had substantial difficulty with this task. Liben explained her results in terms of a distinction between two develop-

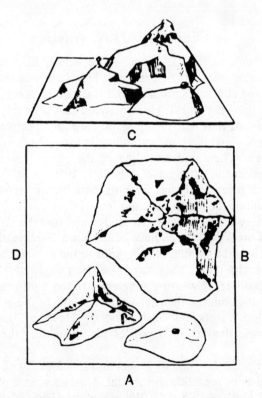

FIG. 4.1   The three-mountains task (from Piaget & Inhelder, 1956, p. 211).

mental levels of knowledge about visual perception put forward by Flavell, Everett, Croft, and Flavell (1981) that build upon Piaget and Inhelder's proposal. At a "Level 1", young children may infer that another's viewpoint does not coincide with their own although they egocentrically do not recognise how these viewpoints are different. At a "level 2", not only do children know that others have different viewpoints of simultaneously visible objects but they can now indicate how these viewpoints differ.

As evidence, Flavell and his co-workers requested 3-year-olds to report the appearance of an object visible to the self and experimenter in upside-down and rightside-up perspectives. For example, the children were shown a horizontally placed picture of a worm lying between a red blanket and a blue blanket. They were asked to say how the worm appeared to the experimenter, who was seated opposite, i.e., if it was lying on the red or the blue blanket. Three-year-olds did not show clear evidence of Level 2 understanding in this study. However, it was tacitly assumed that they shared the purpose and meaning of the language used in the experiment. Should their interpretation differ from that of the experimenter, their lack of success may not be due to a conceptual limitation.

As in the case of conservation, many complications stand in the way of accepting the account of Piaget and the more recent variation offered by Flavell. One of the simplest and most elegant re-examination of children's perspective-taking was carried out by Borke (1975). Children aged 3 and 4 years were shown objects on a rectangular turntable, including a replica of the three-mountains task and a display consisting of a small lake with a toy sailboat, a miniature horse and cow, and a model of the house. They were introduced to Grover, a Sesame Street character, and told, "Grover is going to play this game with us. He will drive his car along the road. Sometimes Glover likes to stop and look out of his car . . .. When Grover stops to look out of his car, I want you to turn the scene that moves so you are looking at it the same way Grover is." On test situations, Grover was parked at each of the three sides which presented a view different from the child's. The task was to turn the display to match Grover's perception.

The children in Borke's experiment were able to answer questions about others' visual perception of objects. The majority could perform successfully on all the displays, except for 3-year-olds on the three-mountains task. Borke's interpretation was that toy figures can be discriminated more easily than the configurations of the three-mountains. Her results would appear to contradict Piaget and Inhelder's contention that young children are incapable of taking others' viewpoints, or Flavell's position that 3- and 4-year-olds at "Level 1" do not recognise how alternative viewpoints differ.

Using toys and other props, DeLoache (1987) has argued that there is a sense in which children's ability to represent the locations of objects in space changes very rapidly and abruptly. In a first experiment, 2 groups of 16 children, the first with a mean age of 31 months and the other with a mean age of 38 months, were shown a furnished room and its scale model located in an adjoining room. An experimenter explicitly described the correspondence between the two toys to be hidden and the furniture that served as hiding places. The children were told that the larger toy was in the "same place" as the miniature toy that was concealed by the furniture of the scale model. They had four trials to retrieve the larger toy from the room. An impressive difference emerged between the two age groups. The older children could retrieve the object very well in the analogous location while few of the younger ones could do so. Yet both age groups could retrieve the miniature toy in the original scale model at the end of each trial, providing evidence that the younger children had not simply forgotten the original hiding place. In a second experiment, children with a mean age of 31 months could use a photograph to retrieve a toy successfully in the room but still could not use the scale model.

According to DeLoache, children under 3 years may not be able to maintain a dual orientation to a model, treating it only as an object rather than a symbol. Since the children's success at using a symbol to find an object changed so abruptly with age, she proposed a maturational explanation. Even so, there are at least three possible reservations to accepting this interpretation of a conceptual limitation with an allegedly maturational underpinning.

First, no attention was devoted to the usual child care environment. Quite possibly, all of the older children were "veterans" in day care while the younger ones were newly enrolled. Since the quality and quantity of daycare has an effect on children's understanding of persons and situations (see Chapter Five for a further discussion), the younger ones may have been uncomfortable in following the instructions of a strange adult who continually referred to an unfamiliar type of model.

Secondly, even if this was not the case for some children, it may have been that the younger ones were mostly correct on the first trial and tired under repeated questioning. They may have been uncertain of the answer in the first place and induced to respond inconsistently, they may have perceived the experimenter's repeated requests as insincere, or the task to be unattractive (Explanations One and Two in Chapter Two). Therefore, rapid changes in representing the model as a symbolic guide to locate objects may be seen as rapid changes in understanding departures from conversational rules.

Thirdly, again with respect to possible violations of rules for communication, young children may not share the experimenter's meaning of the "same place". Once they entered the room, the miniature hiding place of the model was absent and the experimenter's instructions may have been seen as ambiguous and irrelevant. While the children's knowledge of "the same" was examined through (undefined) "independent comprehension checks", these may not have been sufficient to ensure that the children did understand the meaning.

Owing to the unprobed effects of children's understanding of conversational rules and their perceptions of tasks that require the representation of objects, the conclusions which can be drawn from research in this area remain uncertain. Nevertheless, by the age of 4 years, children certainly do have some capacity to represent different perspectives and viewpoints. Not only can they identify that someone else has a different perspective but at times children as young as three can indicate the nature of different perspectives. This amounts to stating that they may display what Flavell has termed Level 2 knowledge.

Even at an age of 1–1½ years, children are non-egocentric in that they shift perspectives in early communication. For example, deaf children acquiring sign languages must learn a mirror-image transformation in order to use the signs for "you" and "me". According to Petitto (1986), these children do not first egocentrically sign "me" for "you" in confusing another's perspective for their own. The errors that are made derive from an overgeneralisation of abstract uses of language. For example, a child may sign "you" for "me", treating "you" as a pronoun with a stable referent, the self.

UNDERSTANDING THE MENTAL WORLD

Therefore, despite Piaget's notion of egocentrism, young children may after all have some knowledge of the properties of objects viewed from alternative perspectives. They understand that the visual perception of others often does not correspond with their own and they may represent the location of concealed objects even if they may not actually employ this understanding in their responses to experimenters' questions. Yet proficiency in visual perspective-taking ability may not easily be generalised to understanding the mental states of others for it cannot be assumed that the requirements for perspective-taking are identical in the social and physical realms.

Glick (1978) and Shultz (1982a) point out that, although the differences between the physical world and the world of persons are not as clear-cut as they may seem, the behaviour of objects is often more stable than that of persons. The social behaviour of persons is only known probabilistically. Sustained interaction between persons is a key focus of social behaviour. Persons both create and react to external events and may be more sensitive to contexts than is the behaviour of objects.

Still, regardless of these apparent differences between social and physical or non-social cognition, young children have at times proved themselves adept at judging perspectives in social settings. In a study of 2- and 3-year-olds, Denham (1986) correlated cognitive and "affective" measures of perspective-taking with observers' ratings of children's social responsiveness and concern for others. The correlations were moderate and inconsistent across measures and were based on small numbers of children. But the important point is that performance on both types of perspective-taking measures was significantly above chance. On the cognitive perspective-taking task, puppets enacted stories in which one puppet had arrived late and lacked privileged information about how the late-arriving puppet would respond in the situation. The children were able to show how the puppet who lacked the information would behave (i.e., by searching in the wrong place for his or her mate). On the affective task, children could indicate how a puppet would feel in a particular story situation (e.g., happy or sad to come to day care, afraid or pleased to see a doctor). After having heard a story, they could affix the appropriate label on the puppet's face from a choice of "happy, sad, angry, and afraid". Their answers were frequently opposite to those which mothers had reported that the children themselves would feel in the same situations. This early understanding of emotions is in keeping with an understanding of what others see.

Harris, Donnelly, Gaz, and Pitt-Watson (1986) have gone a step further in demonstrating many young children have the insight that people may express an emotion which does not correspond to what they really feel. Children aged 4, 6, and 10 years listened to stories such as: "Diana wants to go to her friend's party tonight but she has a tummy ache. She knows that if she tells her mom that she has a tummy ache, her mom won't let her go. She tries to hide how she feels so that her mom will let her go." The children are then asked, "How did Diana really feel, very happy or a bit happy, or very sad or a bit sad?" (a four-point scale). "How did Diana look when that happened to her? Did she look very happy or a bit happy, or very sad or a bit sad?" When questioned further, the 4-year-olds did not easily articulate justifications for their responses. However, they were as proficient as the older subjects in using the experimenter's scale of alternatives to distinguish between how story characters would look and really feel.

A "THEORY OF MIND" IN THE CHILD?

Although adults often talk about concepts in children's minds, to claim that children have a "theory" or "theories of mind" presupposes that there is a valid theory that can be clearly defined. Yet what "mind" actually is remains an issue of ongoing controversy. In essence, experimental research subsumed under the rubric of "theory of mind" has dealt with three major questions: (1) Do children have a knowledge of mental states? (2) Do they understand the distinction between appearance and reality? (3) Do they know that their beliefs may be different from the false beliefs of others?

Do Children Have a Knowledge of Mental States?

In keeping with their ability to identify mechanisms of physical causality, young children have been shown to have a knowledge of brain functions. Much of this work comes from the prolific research of Henry Wellman and his co-workers. Based on a series of clever studies, Johnson and Wellman (1982) reported that kindergarten children understand that the brain is located in the head and is required for mental acts such as thinking, knowing, and—contrary to Piaget (as seen in the last chapter)—dreaming. They differ from older children and adults in believing that the brain is not required for sleep, and for senses such as seeing and hearing, and for involuntary movements such as blinking. For young children, the brain is broadly identified with intelligence. Later in childhood it is regarded as necessary for all mental acts and involuntary acts. By the age of 10 or 11 years, children distinguish between the brain and mind. They refer to the brain as a material organ and to the mind as an immaterial source of voluntary acts.

Age differences in children's knowledge may not so much reflect the lifting of an early conceptual limitation as a growing explicit awareness of mental processes. Indeed, there is evidence that children use mental terms very early in language acquisition. Shatz, Wellman, and Silber (1983) recorded the natural occurrence of words such as "think", "dream", "remember", and "pretend" in 2- and 3-year-olds. By the age of 3, children were using these words to contrast the mental world with a real one. Their sensitivity to mental states was marked by utterances such as "It's not real, I was just pretending", or "I thought the socks were in the drawer, except they weren't".

More recently, Wellman and Estes (1986) have provided firmer evidence that young children are aware of the ontological distinction between the mental world and objective reality. For example, children aged 3 to 5 years were given pairs of "mental-real contrasts". They were asked to compare a boy who was given a cookie with a boy who thought (or remembered, pretended, or dreamed) about a cookie. Even the 3-year-olds correctly chose the boy who could see the cookie, could touch the cookie, and could eat the cookie, and they also were able to say which boy could let a friend eat the cookie or save the cookie and eat it later. Children in the same age range were also given items that could be real (e.g., a dog that rolls over, an ant crawling on the ground) or imaginary (a dog that flies, an ant riding a bicycle). After each item, they were asked four questions: "(1) Have you ever seen (item)? (2) Really, are there (item)? (3) Can you close your eyes and think about (item)? (4) Could you have a dream about (item)?" The great majority of responses were correct regardless of the age of the child. Unlike imaginary items, real items were ones that could be seen and not merely thought or dreamt about.

Do Children Understand the Distinction Between Appearance and Reality?

Despite the evidence that 3-year-olds understand the difference between the mental world and reality, the case has been put that they have little or no understanding of the distinction between appearance and reality. In a very extensive series of experiments in Stanford, California, Flavell, Green, and Flavell (1986) attempted to build on the earlier research that was noted at the end of Chapter Two. They have reported that 3-year-olds are limited in their ability to distinguish between the true nature of a substance and its appearance under, for example, coloured filters or masks and costumes.

For example, in a first study, the participants were 24 children with a mean age of 3 years, 8 months (range 3-3 to 4-0). As part of the testing, they were given familiar or "easy" appearance-reality tasks. For example, milk was shown in a glass with a red filter wrapped around it. The children were asked, "What colour is the milk really and truly? Is it really and truly red or really and truly white? Now here is the second question. When you look at the milk with your eyes right now, does it look white or does it look red?" Care was taken to randomise the order of the alternatives presented so that the children's responses could not simply be a matter of repeating back the last alternative.

Of the 24 children, only 11 correctly identified the milk to look red but to be white really and truly. Similarly, in a second study, an experimenter questioned 3-year-olds on numerous tasks including one in which an adult female is seen to put on a disguise as a bear. The children were asked, "When you look at her with your eyes right now, does she look like Ellie or does she look like (for example) a bear? Here is a different question. Who is over there really and truly? Is she really and truly Ellie or is she really and truly a bear?" Only 52% (a chance level) of responses on the disguise tasks were correct. Two types of errors were equally common on this task: to say that the adult both looked like and truly was a bear, a phenomenism error, or that she looked like and truly was Ellie, a realism error.

Of course, phenomenism (reporting appearance when asked for reality) and realism (reporting reality when asked for appearance) might indicate that some children may misinterpret the experimenter's purpose to test whether they understand the distinction between appearance and reality. Should they applaud the effectiveness of a disguise, they may give phenomenism answers and report on the appearance of an object when asked for reality. Should they perceive the disguise to be ineffective, they may give "realism" answers to both questions. Yet work in England on the early understanding of false beliefs would seem to corroborate the findings of Flavell and his co-workers.

Do Children Know That Their Beliefs May Be Different From the False Beliefs of Others?

Perner, Leekam, and Wimmer (1987, Study Two) saw 32 children with a mean age of 3 years 5 months (range 3-1 to 3-9). Each child together with a friend was taken to a room. The experimenter promised to show each individually what was in a box inside the room and told the friend to wait outside for a turn later. Inside the room with the door closed, the children saw a Smarties box. Even though they thought it contained Smarties candies, they saw that the box had a pencil in it. The children were asked a control question for memory, "Can you remember what's inside here?" (correct response: pencil), and two test questions: (1) "But what did you think was in here?" (correct response: Smarties) and (2) "What will (name of friend) think is in here?" (correct response: Smarties).

Although most were able to answer the first question that referred to one's own false belief, only about half on the second question were able correctly to attribute a false belief to the other child. Perner and his colleagues claimed that, while young children can engage in pretend play, only those older than 3 years consistently possess knowledge of the distinction between appearance and reality and can assign "conflicting truth value" in understanding how others may entertain false beliefs.

Leslie (1987) has gone even further. On the basis of the Perner study, he has contended that, although 3-year-olds have ideas about the existence of mental states, they do not understand the way in which mental states form part of the "causal fabric of the world" in that these are abstract entities which nevertheless have concrete causes and effects.

Yet there are several other possibilities. First, some children may have switched their response from question to question (pencil, Smarties, pencil) in an effort to accommodate the experimenter. Second, other children may have interpreted the final test question to mean "After he (or she) sees it, what will (name of friend) think is in here?" After all, why would a grown-up ask this question unless the information will be shared with all children waiting their turns? In keeping with conversational rules, children may be assigning their own perception of relevance to questions on false beliefs.

Wellman and Bartsch (1988) have suggested a third possibility. They have argued that 3-year-olds often do understand how false beliefs lead to actions. Instead, the difficulty lies in the understanding of "explicit" false beliefs. For example, children can be asked to respond to stories in which a character explicitly desires to find an object which is really in one location, but the character believes that it is in another (wrong) location: "Jane wants to find her kitten. Jane's kitten is really in the playroom. Jane thinks her kitten is in the kitchen." When asked "Where will Jane look for her kitten?" many 3-year-olds answer, "In the playroom" instead of "In the kitchen." Wellman and Bartsch's interpretation of this result was that, when belief and desire are in conflict, children choose on the basis of desire. Again, though, it may be that they assign their own perception of relevance to the test question. They can interpret it to mean, "Where will Jane have to look to find the cat?" and end up by answering this question rather than the one that the experimenter assumed to have asked. They may not understand that the experimenter's purpose is to determine whether children understand false beliefs and are unaware of the need to consider the unspoken but critical implication in the original question that means, "Where will Jane look for her kitten first of all?"

Certainly, however, the most extreme stance has been taken by Perner and Ogden (1988) who advocate a fourth possibility. They have proposed that 3-year-olds' understanding of internal states makes no provision for mental representation whatsoever, based on the results of an experiment designed to compare children's abilities to infer knowledge of a surprise (termed a "representational" state) and hunger (a "non-representational" state) from two story situations. Most of their 3-year-old subjects were able to infer hunger but few were able to infer knowledge of a surprise. Perner and Ogden contended that young children have no notion of representational thought and that they are not easily able to theorise about the mental world. Yet once more this conclusion is unconvincing because the two stories made different demands on children's sensitivity to the conversational rules to be relevant and avoid ambiguity.

Consider, first, the nature of the stories. In the "hunger" story, a mother goes to the shop to buy something (fish and chips) for her very hungry boys. She tells one boy that he can get his dinner because he has clean hands but that the other cannot eat because he has dirty hands. The children in the experiment are shown a picture of the boy with clean hands who has finished his dinner and the boy with dirty hands who has a full plate still on the table. They are asked to say (after a series of memory control questions) who is still hungry.

By contrast, in the "knowledge" story, a mother goes to the shop to buy something (a surprise) for her two boys who are described as very good. Again the mother distinguishes between a boy with clean hands who is told he can look in the box to see the surprise, and a boy with dirty hands who is told he cannot look. Having seen a picture of the mother tilting the box towards the boy with clean hands and away from the boy with dirty hands, the children in the experiment were asked to say (after a series of memory control questions) who knows the secret.

Most of the 3-year-olds correctly chose the boy with dirty hands as the answer to the test question on the hunger story. Performance on the knowledge story was variable with several children giving uninformative "don't know" or double guess ("both boys") responses.

Perner and Ogden evidently assumed that children would share the experimenter's intent to test their ability to ascribe internal states. A major premise was that they would believe that characters in stories listen to their mothers regardless of the situation. Nevertheless, children may interpret the story characteristics differently than intended. In the hunger story, the boy with dirty hands is very likely to eat by touching whereas in the knowledge story he can look perfectly well at the surprise without touching. What if 3-year-olds assume that the boy with dirty hands looks at the surprise despite his mother's request but does not touch, especially if he has previously been described as very good? In this instance, the boy would not have acted against the spirit of her request. Even though only one boy in the story was described as having been allowed to look in the box, children could sensibly ascribe knowledge of the surprise either to the boy with dirty hands or to both boys, particularly since surprises are inherently uncertain and invite guesswork. From this perspective, children would not share the intent of the experimenter on the knowledge story. The test question is ambiguous.

Why then were older children in the study more likely to ascribe knowledge of the surprise to the boy with clean hands? At the age of three years, children are inexperienced in the pragmatic usage of language in conversations. They may simply assume that experimenters (and mothers) will co-operate in an informative and relevant manner. Yet studies of children's ability to understand access to information require that there be a departure from these rules. Children have to understand that the purpose of the experiment is to test their knowledge of a lack of access to information and yet they would ordinarily expect the mother in the story to disclose information in a co-operative, clear and relevant manner. Therefore, they need to understand why and when conversational rules can be violated deliberately.

Leech (1983, p. 82) has proposed that Grice's Co-operative Principle operates in concert with a "Politeness Principle". This requires polite beliefs to be maximised and impolite beliefs to be minimised towards maintaining "the social equilibrium and the friendly relations which enable us to assume that our interlocutors are being co-operative in the first place." As Brown and Levinson (1987, pp. 4–5) have pointed out, this principle cannot be accorded the same status as the Co-operative Principle since it is not necessary in the production of many patterns of language and "some basic modicum of politeness" is not owed to all. However, the obligation to be polite can involve some deviation from conversational rules (i.e., to be non-redundant and informative in communication) and, to this extent, politeness involves a conversational implicature that influences communication.

With regard to Perner and Ogden's story situations, older children may pay more attention to the polite niceties in information exchange than younger ones. To children guided primarily by Co-operative Principle, having dirty hands is insufficient to negate the sharing of a surprise through looking (though it is enough to negate the sharing of food through touching). Because dirty hands is not incompatible with looking, they may not recognise the experimenter's intent in restricting information in the knowledge story to the boy with dirty hands and ascribe to this boy a knowledge of the surprise. A recognition of the experimenter's intent may develop later. With increasing experience in conversations, children may come to understand, as do adult speakers, when rules such as that to be informative in sharing information can be deliberately violated with politeness.

Perner and Ogden attributed successful performance on the hunger story to an early ability to infer a state of "satiation" that does not involve mental representation. However, the procurement of nutrients is an activity that is a prerequisite for fitness and survival and, as noted in Chapter One, many organisms are constrained to learn strategies towards achieving fitness. Children may be especially adept at ascribing states of hunger. They may be constrained towards understanding satiation states and mental representations that are closely connected to these states. For example, with regard to food and contamination, there are many substances that appear safe but are often harmful in reality. As will be seen, even 2-year-olds are often capable of distinguishing between these.

DISTINGUISHING BETWEEN APPEARANCE AND REALITY

Flavell, Perner, and their co-workers have claimed that the 3-year-old has a conceptual deficit in "knowing how" appearance and reality may be discrepant. But in this controversial area, enough reservations persist to suggest otherwise. The problem may be rather one of "knowing when" to employ the knowledge that already exists. We have reported evidence that children often understand the distinction between appearance and reality with respect to common liquids and are able to make inferences and attributions for the false beliefs and answers of others. In these three experiments, we aimed to allow the children to respond in an atmosphere guided by conversational rules.

In our Experiment One (Siegal, Share, & Robinson, 1989), the participants were 48 3-year-olds (range 35 to 47 months, mean age 42 months) seen in individual sessions. Following the procedures used in the previous Flavell studies, all children initially received pretests for language and memory to ensure that the terms used by the experimenter were understood. The testing itself consisted of three phases:

1. Labelling. This AR task was the milk-colour labelling problem used by Flavell, Green, and Flavell (1986, Study One) as part of a series of 24 measures. An experimenter showed the children a clear glass of milk. She poured the contents into a blue-filtered glass so that only a blue liquid was visible and asked, "What colour is the milk really? Is it truly white or truly blue?" (Reality question.) "When you look with your eyes right now, what colour is the milk? Does it look white or look blue?" (Appearance question.)

2. Inferences. In this phase, the children were asked to make inferences based on the false phenomenist beliefs of a friend who did not share AR information. They were shown two glasses and told: "Here is some milk in a blue glass. It looks like juice but it is truly milk. Here is some cream in a clear glass. It looks like milk but isn't really. If a friend came along to ask you for a glass of milk, which one would you give her?" (Reality question.) "Which one would the friend think was milk?" (Appearance question.)

3. Causal attributions. Half the children responded to the story: "A grown-up poured milk into a blue glass with a blue lid on top. She asked Sally, a girl your age, what colour the milk was truly. Sally said the milk was truly blue. Did she say that because she really and truly thought that the milk was blue or was she pretending?" The other half responded to a story that was the same except that a girl said the milk was truly white. The actual names of the story characters in the experiment were the same sex as the children.

To control for order effects, the three phases were counterbalanced across children in the six possible orders. As well, the orders of the questions and alternatives were counterbalanced within each phase.

As shown in Table 4.1, the numbers of those who answered both AR questions correctly in the labelling and inferences phases were above what would be expected by chance alone. There were no significant order effects. All children attributed pretending to the response that milk in a blue glass is blue in reality and a true belief to the response that the milk is white.

TABLE 4.1

Percentages of Responses to the Appearance and Reality Questions in the Labelling and Inference Phases of Experiment One (From Siegal, Share, & Robinson, 1989). The Numbers of Children (Out of 48) are in Parentheses

	Labelling	Inferences
Correct on both	85 (41)	71 (34)
Appearance answers to both questions (phenomenism)	8 (4)	10 (5)
Reality answers to both questions (realism)	4 (2)	15 (7)
Incorrect on both	2 (1)	4 (2)

In Experiment Two, responses on a single AR task were compared with those on multiple tasks under a prolonged form of questioning that children are liable to perceive as contravening the conversational rules to be non-redundant, sincere, relevant and informative. Forty-eight children were assigned to one of two conditions. In a single task condition, half (range 38 to 46 months, mean age 43 months) were given the milk-colour labelling task as in Experiment One. In a multiple task condition, the remainder (range 39 to 47 months, mean age 43 months) responded to AR questions on four groups of four labelling tasks; here the milk-colour task always followed at least one other. The presentation of the task groups was counterbalanced in the 24 possible orders.

As predicted (see Table 4.2), 18 out of 24 children answered both AR questions correctly on the milk-colour task in the single condition. Yet only 10 out of 24 were correct in the multiple condition; many responded that milk in a blue glass is blue in reality as well as appearance. Six of the children in the multiple condition received a colour AR task first (i.e., a

TABLE 4.2

Percentages of Responses on the Milk-colour AR Task in Experiment Two (From Siegal, Share, & Robinson, 1989). The Numbers of Children (Out of 24) are in Parentheses

	Single-task	Multiple-task (Prolonged Questioning)
Correct on both	75 (18)	42 (10)
Appearance answers to both questions (phenomenism)	25 (6)	42 (10)
Reality answers to both questions (realism)	0	13 (3)
Incorrect on both	0	4 (1)

pink kangaroo under a blue filter) and almost all (5/6) were correct. Of the 18 who received the same task later, only 5 succeeded. There was a significant negative relationship between the ordinal position of the tasks and correct responses on both AR questions. In fact, when the AR tasks were presented in the last and next-to-last positions (in the 15th and 16th orders), no child was correct on both questions. Toward the end of a lengthy session of prolonged questioning, a few children may have been so muddled that they answered incorrect on both appearance and reality questions.

In further support of the position that unconventional questioning can impair communication, each child was asked at the conclusion of the session, "Would you like to stop now or go on?" Only 2 children in the single condition declined to proceed in contrast to 10 in the multiple condition.

We devised a follow-up experiment (Siegal & Share, 1990, Experiment 2) to determine whether even younger children may have an implicit knowledge of the distinction between appearance and reality. Information about food such as its taste is conveyed through touch, and representational ability for tactile information is present in very early childhood (Flavell, Flavell, & Green, 1989; Gibson & Walker, 1984; see also the experiments on infants discussed in Chapter One). For this reason, 2-year-olds may be knowledgeable about appearance and reality in the case of food, especially in employing the early contamination sensitivity that was discussed in the last chapter.

The 48 children in this experiment ranged in age from 30 to 42 months, with a mean age of 35 months. Six others were not included, five of whom were silent during questioning and one who indicated a dislike for jam or vegemite (a pungent, popular Australian breakfast spread).

The children were first shown jars of vegemite and jam and asked to say which one, if either, they liked to eat more. All but two preferred the vegemite. They were then randomly assigned in equal numbers to one of two conditions. Owing to the more limited attention and memory of the 2-year-olds, the procedure only required children to label a slice of bread as edible or not. In the experimental condition (age range = 31–41 months, mean = 36 months), they were told as a matter of course during their snack time, "Here's some bread. Oh! it's mouldy." (This statement was delivered in a slightly surprised, non-frightening tone.) The mould did not possess more than a trace odour and, in pilot testing with adults and children, we determined that smell could not be used to detect the presence of concealed mould on bread containing vegemite. Therefore the children could not have been guided in their responses by a persistent odour.

To half of the children, the experimenter said, "Is it OK or not OK to eat?" She spread vegemite (or jam for the two children who preferred jam) over the entire surface of the bread and asked, "Now is the bread OK or not OK to eat?" Since on many cognitive tasks repeated questioning may induce children to switch their responses possibly by suggesting that their initial answer was incorrect, the other children were asked the question only once after the vegemite had been spread.

In the control condition (age range = 30–42 months, mean = 33 months), the children were told as a matter of course during their snack time, "Here's some white bread." Again to half of the children, the experimenter said, "Is it OK or not OK to eat?" She spread vegemite on the entire surface and asked all the children, "Now is the bread OK or not OK to eat?"

Children in the experimental condition rejected the mouldy bread with vegemite at a level above what would be expected by chance. Of the 24 children, 20 (10 out of 12 in each of the single question and repeated question subgroups) rejected the bread when the mouldy portion had been concealed by vegemite; 10 out of 12 consistently rejected the bread on both questionings. By contrast, out of the 24 children in the control condition, only 3 (1 in the single question subgroup and 2 in the repeated question subgroup) rejected the white bread with vegemite that was free of mould; no child in this condition consistently rejected the bread on both questionings. Even those as young as 30 months were able to identify an apparently edible substance as not good to eat.

The results of our three experiments do not address the issue of processes by which children seek out AR distinctions. Outside familiar areas such as food, AR knowledge may be more fragile. In addition, the false belief questions in our Experiment One differed somewhat from those employed by Perner and his colleagues.

Bearing these considerations in mind, 3-year-olds in natural conversation overall demonstrated a clear understanding of the distinction between appearance and reality with regard to common foods and liquids. Not only could they indicate that a drink which looks blue in appearance is white in reality, but they were able to make inferences and attributions for others' false beliefs and answers. Even 2-year-olds may have an implicit understanding of the distinction between reality and the phenomenal world of appearances. The children's performance indicates more that a rote understanding, and provides further support for my position that they abstract concepts of the properties of objects.

While these findings cast doubt upon the presence of a conceptual limitation that is rooted in phenomenism and realism, AR knowledge may not be explicitly disclosed in reaction to forms of questions that are liable to contravene the quantity and relevance rules. Such forms can involve a repeated or prolonged series of questions, or other cases where children perceive questions to have answers that are obvious, silly, pointless, or impossible to obtain.

In response to AR questions, children may answer incorrectly in evaluating the effectiveness of the experimenter's attempts at providing deceptive appearances. Especially during unconventional or prolonged questioning on AR colour tasks, they may be induced to say that an apparent deception is so good that it is real; hence, milk really and truly is blue when placed under a blue filter. The unconventional nature of such questioning and the child's lack of experience with the purpose of these procedures renders this possibility a good one. A similar account can be given for a realism pattern on object identity tasks. For example, should 3-year-olds evaluate a sponge which apparently looks like a rock as a less than adequate facsimile, they could quite justifiably respond both that the object looks like a sponge and is a sponge in reality. Indeed, as shown in our Experiment Two, after having experienced prolonged questioning on AR tasks, many children if given the opportunity would choose not to proceed any further. This scenario is illustrated in Fig. 4.2.

The effects of prolonged or other forms of unconventional questioning on children's responses may also occur on AR training tasks as well as on measures of false beliefs and perspective-taking. While Flavell, Green, Wahl, and Flavell (1987) have reported that attempts to train children's AR knowledge are largely unsuccessful, many training tasks can also involve unconventional questioning. Training may be ineffective for that reason. How methods of questioning influence children's responses on measures related to AR knowledge is unclear and obviously requires further study.

CHILDREN'S TESTIMONY

What of the applied side to research on children's understanding of appearance and reality and the false beliefs of others? For example, can they use their knowledge to provide accurate testimony?

As one step in this direction. Yuill and Perner (1987) have examined perspective-taking abilities in traffic accident situations. Children aged 6 to 9 years and adults were given 4 stories involving a collision between a protagonist (e.g., a cyclist) who had the right of way and another road user who was a minor character (e.g., a car motorist). In each of two sessions, an experimenter read story pairs and asked the children to attribute blame for the accident. Both story pairs contrasted a cyclist who knew that the motorist did not know she was approaching with a cyclist who mistakenly thought that the motorist did know. In one of the pairs, the motorist was described as knowing about the approach of the cyclist and in the other pair he was described as ignorant.

FIG. 4.2   A child giving an appearance answer when asked to report reality: an illustration of the possible context of "phenomenism" errors on an appearance–reality task which children perceive to be unattractive.

The four versions of the stories were as follows: This story is about two people going along a street, Dan and Cathy. Dan is sitting in his car. He is just going to get out of his car. Cathy is coming up from behind the car on her bicycle. Before Dan opens the car door, he looks out of the window to see whether he has room to get out.

1. KNOW (NOT KNOW): but he doesn't look round far enough back, so he doesn't see Cathy coming up from behind. Cathy sees that he didn't look back, so she knows that he has not seen her at all.
2. THINK (KNOW): but he doesn't look round far enough back, so he doesn't see Cathy coming up from behind. Cathy sees that he looked out and she thinks he must have seen her, but he didn't.
3. KNOW (KNOW): and as he looks out, he can see Cathy coming up from behind. Cathy sees him looking at her and so she knows he has seen her.
4. THINK (NOT KNOW): and as he looks out, he can see Cathy coming up from behind. Cathy doesn't see that he looked that far back, and so she thinks he has not seen her at all, but he has.

Care was taken to ensure that the children remembered and compre-hended the stories. The experimenter used miniature toys and diagrams to act out the stories with the help of the child. The actual names of the story characters were different for each version. After each story, the children answered the question, "How much is Cathy to blame for what hap-pened?" by responding to a 7-point scale (all–very much–quite a lot–in between–a little–a tiny little–not at all). After the second story in each pair, subjects chose the protagonist who was more to blame for the accident.

By the age of 7, many of the children were able to state correctly that a cyclist who knew about the motorist's ignorance was more to blame for the accident than a cyclist who was mistaken. Moreover, in response to descriptions of accidents in which adequate precautions had been taken to avoid harm, even 5-year-olds consider such negligence to lessen but not to absolve culprits of responsibility (Shultz, Wright, and Schleifer, 1986).

Experiments on children's understanding of the knowledge of others may reveal ways by which they can become acquainted with the circum-stances of traffic accidents. For example, an interesting study would be to give 5- to 7-year-olds a task where they could state simply whether the responses of others as witnesses to traffic accidents were correct and whether the movements of persons under simulated traffic conditions would result in a collision.

In a court of law, children's testimony has been used to corroborate adults' attributions of blame (Goodman, Golding, & Haith, 1984). It may be a popular misconception that children's memory is necessarily more susceptible to distortion than that of adults. Johnson and Foley (1984) have pointed out that, while children may have difficulty recalling the details of adult conversations and may produce less detailed courtroom evidence than adults, they may be able to recognise who did what. They may be as proficient as adults in describing a sequence of events and where these took place. Moreover, although children's imagination and lack of experience with strategies for recall may interfere with the reliability of their testimony, they may be without the prejudices that mar the reports of adults. To illustrate, Johnson and Foley have used an example from the work of Allport and Postman (1947). Adults and children viewed a picture of a subway scene. The adults often reported that a black man was holding a razor in an aggressive way. But in reality, it was a white man. If children remembered that a man was holding a razor, they never confused who it was.

Perhaps the most detailed examination to date of children's susceptibility to leading questions has been carried out by Ceci, Ross, and Toglia (1987). In the first of four studies, an experimenter read a picture storybook to 3- to 9-year-olds in groups of 10 to 20 children. The story was about a girl named Lauren who had a stomach-ache from eating her eggs too quickly on the morning of her first day at school. One day after the story was presented, an experimenter who was usually different than the person who had read the story provided each child with either biased or unbiased information. In the biased condition, the children were asked, "Do you remember the story about Lauren who had a headache because she ate her cereal too fast?" while the question in the unbiased condition was, "Do you remember the story of Lauren, who was sick?" Two days later, an experimenter instructed each child to select the pictures that accompanied the story from choices of Lauren eating eggs and suffering from a stomach-ache paired with the information suggested in the biased information condition, Lauren eating cereal and suffering from a headache. Over 80% of the responses of children who had received unbiased information were correct and there were no significant age differences. By contrast, only 37% of the choices of the 3- to 4-year-olds who had received biased information were correct—significantly fewer than those of the older children.

In subsequent experiments, the suggestibility of the younger children was reduced, though not eliminated, when the bias came from another child rather than an adult. Thus the effects of suggestibility might in part be viewed in terms of a desire to conform to an adult authority figure. Yet an issue that remains unaddressed is whether the presentation of biased information might signal to a child that it is all right to pick a different choice. Moreover, such stories are not equally appealing for all children.

Having heard the two story versions, younger ones might not share the purpose underlying the request to choose between pictures. They may interpret the question to require that they should choose their own food preference and outcome for Lauren. In any event, as Ceci and his colleagues caution, we are still a long way from predicting the behaviour of child witnesses.

While children can be credited with a substantial capacity for representing objects and viewpoints, a major difficulty in research on the ability to judge mental states and others' beliefs and perspectives must be acknowledged. Higgins (1981, p. 133) is one researcher who has alleged that many of these tasks do not actually require inferential skills. He has maintained that "judgements involve role-taking when there is an inference about a target's viewpoint (or response) under circumstances where the judge's own viewpoint is salient and different from the target's." The tasks used by Denham, Harris, and others, discussed earlier, did not require children to inhibit or control their own responses in subjugating them to the viewpoints of others. In some "perspective-taking" situations, children attach labels to targets and no inference may be necessary. They judge thoughts, emotions and feelings as if they themselves were in the situations and not someone else whose viewpoint actually differs. Similarly, in Ceci's measures of suggestibility, children may have been offering their own choice of alternatives even though they have the ability to recall the initial story. According to Higgins, perspective-taking ought to involve the capacity to subjugate the salient, intrusive viewpoint of the self to the opposing viewpoint of others.

As Higgins (1981) has pointed out, role-taking consists of the ability to interrelate multiple factors and to control one's own viewpoint. Contrary to a Piagetian analysis, many children can interrelate and represent different points of view. Thus in judging the perspectives of others, an increase with age in performance is probably due to accumulated social knowledge.

For example, Higgins, Feldman, and Ruble (1980) examined the ability of children and adults to predict the preferences of peers and non-peers with regard to snacks, meals, and activities. The responses of 4- to 5-year-olds were similar to those of 8- and 9-year-olds or adults. Preschoolers did not egocentrically choose their own preferences for peers and non-peers alike. However, the 4- and 5-year-olds were less accurate in specifying non-peers' preferences. Higgins and his colleagues suggest that the preschoolers lack "social category" knowledge about the category of persons whose preferences are to be predicted. They do not know enough about 8- and 9-year-olds or adults to answer questions; neither do they have a prototypical 8- or 9-year-old or grown-up to use as a reference point in making accurate predictions about activity preferences. The unreliability of children's responses on many role-taking tasks may simply be due to their unfamiliarity with a domain of knowledge rather than the absence of a capacity for understanding.

Although role-taking in the sense of Higgins' stringent definition is difficult to establish in children, the extent to which adults use this ability and control one's own viewpoint is also unclear. There is the story of a man who moans to an acquaintance, "My son was in a car accident last week and we don't know whether he'll ever recover." The acquaintance says, "That is terrible. But it could be worse." The man continues, "My daughter has cancer of the pancreas and doesn't have long to live." The acquaintance says, "That's terrible. But it could be worse." The man retorts, "What do you mean it could be worse?" The acquaintance replies, "It could happen to me!"

Many conversations between adults subtly take this form. While children may disguise their own viewpoints less frequently, they can often represent the perspectives of others. In this respect, they may not necessarily be disadvantaged when compared with adults.

5 Understanding Persons

If a parent asks a child, "What did you learn in school today?" the child will often say, "Not much." The reply will also often be "not much" to "Did the teacher read to you?" or "Did you learn more about counting?" But if the question is, "Who got into trouble today?" or "What happened at lunch with your friends?" a wealth of information is obtained. For example, "Kate's mom bought her a beautiful dress" or "Jill can skip up to 50" or "A boy was sent to the principal" or "I got into a fight with Jim" accompanied by a vivid description of the incident. Concerns about friendship, popularity, and sex-appropriate behaviour are highly relevant and can predominate in the minds of very young children.

THE STAGE APPROACH TO CHILDREN'S CONCEPTS OF FRIENDSHIP

Psychologists in the Piagetian tradition have often explained children's understanding of friendship in terms of conceptual limitations. Following Piaget's clinical method, Selman (1980, p. 106) asked children questions such as: What kinds of things do good friends sometimes fight or disagree about? What are some good ways to settle fights or disagreements with a friend? Can friends have arguments and still be friends?

Selman's interview probed for children's understanding of several issues: why and how friendships are made, how friends resolve problems, how friendships break up, and the nature of trust and jealousy in friendships. Without attaching precise age ranges to types of answers, Selman interpreted concepts of friendship at five stages or levels, from 5 years (predominantly Level 0) to late adolescence and adulthood (predominantly Levels 3 and 4):

Level 0: Momentary friendships and physical solutions to conflicts.
Level 1: One-way friendships and unrelated solutions to conflicts.
Level 2: Bilateral friendships and co-operative solutions to conflicts.
Level 3: Stability of friendships and mutual solutions to conflicts.
Level 4: Autonomous interdependence and symbolic action as a resolution to conflicts.

Selman characterised early friendships at Level 0 in terms similar to those which have been used to interpret preschoolers' lack of success on standard conservation and perspective-taking tasks. Children are said to reason about conflict between friends without any reflecting on the psychological effects of a particular strategy for resolution upon either party's feelings or motives. They avoid conflict by separating physically or by moving on to another activity. This level is marked by egocentrism, momentary friendships, and an inability to conceptualise differences in perspective between the self and others.

At Level 1, children view conflicts as problems that are caused by the actions of one party and felt by the other alone. Since they can only conceive of a disagreement as caused by one party, an apology or separation is enough to repair a conflict.

At Level 2, they view conflicts as caused by some external event. The assumption is that a conflict can be resolved independently of a relationship between friends so long as each person is satisfied. At Level 3, there is the understanding that a conflict may originate from the relationship itself. Both sides must accept a mutual resolution that would be satisfactory if the participants changed places. For example, adolescents may claim that, "if you just settle up after a fight that is no good. You gotta really feel that you'd be happy the way things went if you were in your friend's shoes. You can just settle up with someone who is not a friend, but that's not what friendship is really about" (Selman, 1980, p. 111).

Finally, at Level 4, individuals balance personal autonomy with the "close-knit mutality" of friendship. Relations can be "symbolically" repaired by respecting the independence of the other person and keeping channels of communication open when there are conflicts.

Selman formulated these five levels based on interviews with 91 individuals aged from 3 to 34 years. He concluded that concepts of friendship can be analysed according to Piagetian criteria and maintained that interview responses can be described as a "structural whole", a general orientation towards friendship at each level. In addition, he contended that the levels form an invariant sequence in that no individual skips a level or regresses. For Selman, preschoolers' friendships are unstable owing to their basis in physical characteristics and the transitory nature of their play. Young children are egocentric in their peer relations and, with age, they come to understand the viewpoint of others.

The scope of Selman's research is impressive. However, it is mainly dependent on an interview methodology in which children are asked to respond to direct questions about hypothetical (and possibly irrelevant) stories of friends. This accepts a first theoretical leap that young children are conceptually limited as shown by their performance on Piagetian tasks presented in formats where, at least sometimes, they may have misinterpreted the purpose and meaning of the language used by the experimenter. It also accepts a second leap that children's friendships are limited by an inherent egocentrism in their ability to take the role of others. My position is that both these premises are highly questionable.

Indeed, contrary to Selman's proposal, there is evidence that many preschoolers have stable reciprocal friendships and that these are not necessarily tied to physical characteristics. For example, Gershman and Hayes (1983) asked 37 children (mean age = 50 months; range 34 to 61 months) to name a real child at their preschool as "someone you like more than anyone else" and to give justifications for their choices. Out of the 37, 22 (or 11 pairs) could be identified as reciprocal friends through their mutual choices. In observations of their behaviour at preschool, friends spent between 60 and 70% of their time with each other in free play. In a later phase of the study, the children were again asked to name their best friend after a 4 to 6 month interval. Most of those who were initially involved in reciprocal friendships remained stable in that category. Similar studies (e.g., Ladd, Price, & Hart, 1988) have shown that there is substantial consistency in the co-operative behaviour of preschoolers who are preferred as playmates.

In other work, Furman and Bierman (1983) compared methods of studying friendship in children aged 4 to 7 years. Friendship conceptions were measured in three ways: on an open-ended interview, on a picture recognition task, and on a forced-choice rating task. The interview consisted of four questions: "(1) What is a friend? (2) A friend is someone who . . .? (3) Why do people need to have friends? and (4) Tell me what you do with friends?" In the picture recognition task, different activities were shown in pictures and the children were asked to say whether these would promote friendship. The pictures represented five potential bases for friendship: (1) affection (for example, love each other, care for each other); (2) support (help and share with each other); (3) common activities (play and make things together); (4) propinquity (are together a lot, sit by each other); and (5) physical characteristics (wear blue hats, have black hair). Finally, in the forced-choice rating task, the children were shown the pictures again in pairs and were asked to select the activity that it was more important for friends to do.

Significant age differences for both sexes in conceptions of friendship were found only in one specific area. Consistent with Selman's approach, children aged 4 and 5 years were more likely than 6- and 7-year-olds to mention physical characteristics, particularly in their answers to the open-ended interview questions.

However, even on the interview, 63% of the younger children mentioned affection as an aspect of friendship and 53% mentioned support. Moreover, although the children in Furman and Bierman's sample had been enrolled at daycare centres, length of attendance was left unspecified in their research report. Those children who mentioned the more abstract features of friendship may have been daycare veterans who had been provided with the opportunity for intensive peer interaction. While the newly enrolled might identify wearing similar hats as a sign of friendship, this type of choice does not amount to evidence for a conceptual limitation in young children's peer relations. There are occasions when a reliance on physical characteristics is a sensible strategy to enter a group. In fact, it can be employed by adults in new situations such as first time attendance at a professional conference. The same may apply in the case of preschool novices meeting other children for the first time. In any case, as Furman and Bierman point out, apart from the role of physical characteristics in the formation of friendships, ideas about affection and support have not yet been shown to be necessary or sufficient conditions for children to infer that a friendship is present.

McGuire and Weisz (1982) examined the relationship between children's social behaviour and their popularity and friendships. The participants in their study were 293 fourth and fifth graders in rural North Carolina. The children listed their five best friends in order of preference on a questionnaire. Popularity was simply defined in terms of the number of nominations received by each child. Friendship, defined as "chumship", was measured by stable, mutual, best-friend choices; children were assigned membership in a chum group if they had scores above the mean for their sex and grade on a Chumship Checklist, including items such as "Tell each other things you wouldn't tell anyone else" and "Sleep over at each other's house."

In addition, the children were given measures of perspective-taking such as those described in the last chapter, together with measures of "altruism", involving observations of incidents during lunch and recess. Children with chums had higher levels of perspective-taking and observed altruism than did children without chums. Generally, popularity scores did not correlate with perspective-taking or altruism. Nor did perspective-taking itself relate to altruism.

This study is notable in that the authors distinguish between friendship and popularity. From our school years, we know many popular individuals who would have been at times chosen by virtually everyone as persons with whom we would have most liked to spend our time. However, these disgustingly popular persons would not necessarily be regarded as close, intimate friends by anyone in particular. By contrast, even though an unpopular child can have a close friend, children without friends and children who are unpopular tend to be one and the same. The friendless are neglected or even outwardly rejected by their peers. Not surprisingly, they may be less altruistic, less likely to share, co-operate and make friends.

REJECTED AND NON-REJECTED CHILDREN

Selman's clinical interview is based on a Piagetian approach. It is tied into Piaget's theory of cognitive development and proposes that there are serious restrictions in young children's concepts of friendships and capacity for understanding persons. But as we have seen in the last chapter, children have at least some ability to take the role of the other and to infer others' mental states. Moreover, there is little evidence to support the existence of "structural wholes" at various developmental stages or levels. In fact, perspective-taking may be incidental to some other relationship between children's knowledge about persons and their status in the peer group. Their responses in an interview are vulnerable to the perception that conversational rules have been violated. The outcome may be to underestimate their concepts of friendship. Under direct or prolonged questioning in hypothetical interview situations which can lay aside, for example, the quantity and relevance rules, they may be doing little more than responding to please (or even displease) the experimenter.

Let us not be misled by the apparent lack of depth in young children's concepts of friendship. Since they are not necessarily constrained by an inability to share perspectives, it is appropriate to examine the relationship between their knowledge about others and status among peers.

Children who are rejected may have different knowledge and beliefs about others than those who have friends or who are popular. This knowledge may fall short of matching their capacity for understanding. Without the knowledge to develop the skills for dealing effectively with social situations, they may have difficulties in peer relations and in following teachers' directions (Coie & Krehbiel, 1984, p. 1466).

In this respect, a key aspect of children's friendships consists of the skill to anticipate and evaluate the consequences of behaviour that lead to acceptance in the peer group (Dodge, 1985). According to Turiel's (1983) account, to anticipate and evaluate consequences involves the ability to distinguish between different types of transgressions. By the age of 4 to 5 years, children can distinguish between violations of "social" conventions which are arbitrarily defined with reference to a particular setting, and violations of moral prohibitions that are intrinsically wrong irrespective of the setting (Smetana, 1981; 1985). For instance, they are likely to regard transgressions such as injuring another child as morally wrong even if no punishment or prohibition existed. Violations such as not placing a toy in a designated spot or calling a teacher by the first name are likely to be regarded as transgressions tied to arbitrary settings. Outside these contexts, these acts would be permissible.

Importantly, in keeping with conversational rules, questions about different types of transgressions are likely to be perceived as clear, sincere, and relevant to children's concerns. As demonstrated in a variety of studies, preschoolers distinguish between the gravity of these two types of violations in commenting on actual behaviour. (Nucci & Turiel, 1978; Nucci & Nucci, 1982; Peery, 1979). For example, children who have witnessed social transgressions respond permissively to questions such as "What if there wasn't a rule in the school about (the observed act), would it be all right to do it then?" and seldomly react at all. But they frequently react to moral transgressions by expressions of emotion, injury, or loss. This distinction demonstrates that they possess concepts of right and wrong; they do not adhere simply to a doctrine that all transgressions are equally serious and punishable.

In earlier work (Siegal & Storey, 1985), we showed that daycare veterans who had been enrolled in child care centres for at least 18 months more clearly distinguished between moral and social transgressions than did a group of newly enrolled children with similar verbal intelligence scores. Compared to the newly enrolled, veterans judged social violations to be less naughty and worthy of punishment. However, the relationship between children's ideas about transgressions and their acceptance or rejection by other children is unclear. Recently, we attempted to explore this issue (Sanderson & Siegal, 1988). The preschoolers in our study were classified in five peer status groups: controversial; popular; average; neglected; and rejected.

It has often been noted (Coie & Kupersmidt, 1983; Coie, Dodge, & Coppotelli, 1982; Dodge, Coie, & Brakke, 1982; French & Waas, 1985; Hartup, 1983; Hymel, 1983; Ladd, 1983) that popular children are received positively by their peers while the rejected are rebuffed in reaction to inappropriate approach behaviours. Controversial children produce high rates of prosocial and aggressive behaviour. They are skilled at eliciting both highly positive and negative reactions from others. Neglected children display low rates of behaviour and can be inept with peers, though the interaction they do show frequently resembles that of others.

On this basis, we hypothesised that controversial and popular children, with their superior social skills, would have the most highly developed knowledge and would distinguish most clearly between social and moral transgressions. By contrast, since unpopular preschoolers are more likely to transgress (Furman & Masters, 1980) and rejected children possess fewer social skills than their popular and controversial peers (Dodge, 1983), we predicted that the distinction between the gravity of social and moral transgressions should be unclear in this group.

The children in our study were 102 4- and 5-year-olds (51 boys and 51 girls) in full-time attendance for a mean of 19½ months at five child care centres located in middle class districts. Their ages ranged from 48 months to 68 months with a mean of 53 months. Twelve other children were excluded because parental consent had not been given. The centres provided continuous care for children between the ages of 2 and 5 years.

Each child was seen individually by a female experimenter during a session lasting approximately 10 to 15 minutes. He or she was given instances of moral and social transgressions followed by a peer nomination task to determine his or her status among others.

Questions About Transgressions. The children were presented with the same six items that we used in a previous study (Siegal & Storey, 1985, Study Two). The three moral transgressions involved: (1) a child hitting another; (2) a child not sharing toys with another child; and (3) a child not helping another who had tripped on the playground. Social transgressions were: (4) a child not putting toys away in the toy box; (5) a child not sitting at story time; and (6) a child eating ice-cream with a fork. The items were presented to the children in a random order.

Four questions were asked on each of the six items. The first question concerned judgements of naughtiness. The child was shown a cardboard sheet with four faces: a happy face (verbally labelled "OK"), a slight frown ("a little bit bad"), a larger frown ("very bad") and a big scowl ("very, very, bad"). Before the questioning, each child demonstrated proficiency in using the scale.

The first question involved a description of the relevant transgression. The children were asked to choose the face from a 4-point scale of naughtiness "that tells me about it". Responses were scored from 1 for "OK" to 4 for "very, very, bad". For the second question, they were asked if the transgressor should be punished. They were then required to indicate whether this should be a little or a lot. Responses were scored on a 0 to 2 scale, with 0 for no punishment, 1 for a little, and 2 for a lot. Question 3 dealt with the "contingency" of transgression. The children were asked whether it would be all right to commit the transgression if the perpetrator did not get into trouble. For question 4 on the "relativity" of the transgression, they were asked if each of the six transgressions would be permissible at home or in another child care centre. Responses on questions 3 and 4 were scored on a 0 to 1 scale ranging from (0) "yes" to (1) "no".

Peer Status Measures.   Before the start of testing, all the children were photographed in small groups of 4 to 6, with girls and boys represented in roughly equal proportions in each photograph. The children were shown the photographs of their child care group. The experimenter pointed to the pictures and named each child successively. She then requested the children to look at all photographs and to nominate the three peers with whom they most liked to play and three with whom they least liked to play.

Peer status was classified by the "binomial probability" method used in an earlier study of fifth graders by Newcomb and Bukowski (1984). The number of nominations each child received from his or her peers on both the like most (LM) and like least (LL) questions was used to calculate social impact scores. These consisted of the total number of nominations the child received on both categories (LM + LL). There were five nominating groups, one from each child care centre. Their sizes were 12, 13, 22, 23, and 29. Rare scores on both the LM and LL questions ranged from 4 and above for the smallest nominating group of 12, to 6 and above for the largest nominating group. A "rare" score on the social impact dimension was identified as consisting of 2 nominations or less.

Using this method, the preschoolers were classified into controversial, popular, average, neglected, and rejected groups consisting of 8, 16, 54, 13, and 11 children respectively. Popular children had a rare LM score plus a score below the mean on LL. Controversial children were identified by a rare score on either one, or both, of the LM or LL dimensions. If the rare score occurred on only one category, then the other score was above the mean. Rejected status was assigned to children with a rare LL score, plus an LM score that was below the mean. Those who were classified as neglected had a lower than chance social impact score. The average group obtained social impact scores at a chance level and did not have rare LL or LM scores.

Peer status had a significant effect only on the amount of punishment due to the perpetrators of transgressions (question 2, see Fig. 5.1), possibly because children regard punishment to be more immediately related to anticipating and evaluating the consequences of behaviour than issues of naughtiness, contingency, and relativity. The four non-rejected groups (controversial, popular, average, and neglected) rated moral transgressions as deserving more punishment then social ones. As predicted, rejected children (who were enrolled for the same length of time as the non-rejected) did not discriminate between the punishment due to moral and social transgressions.

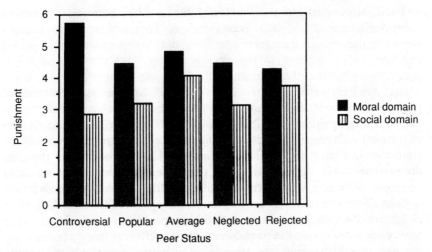

FIG. 5.1   Peer status and punishment assigned to the perpetrators of transgressions (from Sanderson & Siegal, 1988). Scores ranged from 0 to a possible maximum of 6. All status groups, except the rejected, rated violations of moral rules to be significantly worthier of punishment than violations of social convention transgressions.

Except for the item on hitting, the rejected prescribed little punishment for transgressions. In particular, compared to other peers, they tended to regard "not sharing" to be less worthy of punishment. Although the responses on this single item did not differ significantly from those of the other groups, the tendency is consistent with the results of studies indicating that unpopularity is associated with children's lack of reciprocity in sharing rewards (Enright & Sutterfield, 1980; Enright, Enright, & Lapsley, 1981). The rejected may not anticipate the consequences of a refusal to share or they may expect that sharing will not result in a positive outcome in peer relations (Sobol & Earn, 1985; Sobol, Earn, Bennett, & Humphries, 1983). Possibly, the parents of the rejected do not critically differentiate between their children's transgressions. A lack of clarity in childrearing methods may promote the inappropriate or aggressive approach behaviour that is characteristic of rejected children (see Chapter Six for a further discussion.)

Unlike the rejected group, the neglected children differentiated between the punishment due to social and moral transgressions. The scores of the neglected and average groups were similar. Recent studies using older children (e.g., French & Waas, 1985) have found that the behaviour of the neglected resembles that of average ones. The distinction between the rejected and neglected groups is an important one and merits more attention (see Asher & Dodge, 1986; Asher & Wheeler, 1986; Rubin & Mills, 1988). Some children may be neglected by others, not because they feel rejected, but because they choose to be alone.

The controversial group most clearly distinguished between the punishment due to moral and social transgressions. They assigned more punishment to the moral transgressions than did the popular and rejected children and, compared to the average group, they rated social transgressions as meriting less punishment. Although the numbers of controversial children were few, their finely tuned distinction between types of transgressions concurs with the observation that the behaviour of controversials is highly skilled. While the behaviour of controversial children may often meet with negative reactions from peers and reprimands from adults, controversials may engage in even more prosocial behaviour than do popular peers (Dodge, 1983). Their peer interaction may be both more extensive and intensive than that of other children, including those who are popular. The peer status of controversials may be a reflection of high rates of attention-seeking or "manipulation", supported by a sophistication in their knowledge about the punishment due to different transgressions.

Concepts of transgressions are related to both the quality and quantity of peer experience. Contrary to stages derived from Selman's interview technique, the majority of young children responding to questions guided by conversational rules do display a capacity to form more than transitory friendships. This is confirmed by a moderate degree of stability in peer nominations over periods of two weeks or more. Preschoolers have not only been found to place emphasis on affection and support in their friendships; often they have the skill to evaluate the consequences of social behaviours that are ordinarily unacceptable to either adults or other children. A lack of knowledge about persons, rather than a conceptual limitation, may underscore rejection in early childhood.

Nevertheless, this initial study had definite limitations. Our results were based on small numbers of boys and girls, especially in the groups of non-average children. Further, contrary to prediction, the responses of popular and average children were not significantly different. Distinctions between different types of transgressions may be an important but insufficient condition for peer acceptance.

CULTURE AND KNOWLEDGE

What is the influence of culture on children's responses to questions about transgressions? To answer this question, Nisan (1987) compared the judgements of three groups of schoolchildren in a study carried out in Israel: secular middle class Jews from a large city, secular Jews from kibbutzim, and Moslem Arabs from a traditional village. Forty children were in each group; half were 6- and 7-year-olds and half were 10- and 11-year-olds. The children were asked to evaluate behaviours such as taking a toy belonging to another child and calling a teacher by the first name in a country where these behaviours were either prohibited or permitted. Then they were asked to say what the law should be. Compared to the two groups of Jewish children, the traditional Arab group, regardless of age, evaluated both moral and social transgressions more seriously. The great majority of the traditional children maintained that all the transgressions, whether moral or social, should be prohibited by law.

Nisan attributed his results to differences in social norms that are grounded in a general cultural outlook. Turiel, Nucci, and Smetana (1988) have disputed this interpretation. They take issue with the familiarity of the behaviours that Nisan presented to the children and with the nature of the questions and the scoring system used in this study. But what if culture does limit the distinction made? How might peer status be affected? As Nisan (1988) has maintained, even a culturally determined analysis leaves room for children's cognition. The more complex the situation, the more amenable it will be to the influence of both culture and knowledge on their ideas about transgressions. This process and its outcome may be subtle. Even seemingly minute differences in the orientations of children may be significant influences on their friendship and popularity.

In Japan, for example, the belief in the strength of the relationship between an individual's attitude and behaviour is probably considerably weaker than that in Western countries. Compared to their Japanese counterparts, Western children may be more likely to identify occasions where it is wrong to act inconsistently to one's expressed attitude even if one did not get into trouble or nobody cared. In a collective society such as Japan, such violations might be judged less severely; there may be a normative understanding that inconsistency can reflect group solidarity and pressure.

In Japan, as well, individual speakers show deference to preserve the ranking of the group; they seek to humble themselves and to exalt the addressee (Matsumoto, 1988). This norm of group solidarity may be the focus of cultural differences in distinctions between social and moral transgressions. Compared to their Western counterparts, Japanese children may regard peers as wrong not to display the trappings of group solidarity at school (for example, to refuse to join in singing the school anthem) even if they did not get into trouble or nobody cared. If children construe this norm as a moral prohibition, they may reject those who transgress.

Would cross-cultural differences in ideas about transgressions invalidate the position that the social-moral distinction is theoretically useful? Turiel (1989) has pointed out that in many instances overlaps between categories are present and the numbers of marginal cases are large. Yet the categories are still retained. Many books, for example, are a mixture of fiction and non-fiction, but bibliophiles do not discard these terms in categorising books. Similarly, cases exist such as wearing a bikini to the funeral of parent—a transgression which would have both social conventional overtones in style of dress and moral overtones in showing respect for the dead person and mourners. What does matter is that there should be prototypical instances of categories. For example, near unanimity exists that rape and unprovoked killing are moral transgressions.

HUMOUR REPUTATION

Naturally, there are other aspects of popularity and friendship besides ideas about transgressions. For example, peer relations can be influenced by children's physical attractiveness, motor skills, and, especially, their reputation as humorists.

Dodge and Somberg (1987) divided classes of third, fourth, and fifth grade boys into adjusted-nonaggressive and rejected-aggressive groups. In contrast to the adjusted-nonaggressive group, the rejected boys had social preference scores below zero and were rated low on social competence and high on aggression by their peers. The children were shown a set of video-recorded incidents involving a pair of boys in a play activity. The intention of the provocateur in the incidents was portrayed as hostile, accidental, prosocial, or ambiguous. The children were asked to interpret the boy's intention and to indicate how they would respond if the provocation had actually happened to them.

The rejected unjustifiably attributed hostile motives to the actions of boys with accidental or ambiguous intentions and were more likely than their non-aggressive peers to indicate retaliation in cases of accidental provocation. A tendency to overattribute hostile motives in others is of course not limited to children. Adults can do the same, particularly when faced with an unfamiliar culture. For example, tourists during the recent coup in Fiji were heard to misinterpret the native greeting "bula, bula" (hello, hello) as "Put your hand up and give us your wallet."

Just as hostile attributions may produce rejection in children, humorous attributions may be associated with popularity. Masten (1986) investigated the relation of children's "peer reputation" with humour appreciation, comprehension, and production. Fifth graders were asked to assess the funniness of cartoons on a 5-point scale ranging from 1 (not funny at all) to 5 (very, very funny) while, unknown to the subject, an experimenter rated their "mirth" reactions to each cartoon. The children also explained the humour portrayed in the cartoons and produced titles or captions to make a cartoon funnier. After controlling for the effects of IQ, humour appreciation (funniness and mirth) and production were related to a dimension of peer reputation; humourless children were regarded by their peers as withdrawn, shy, or unhappy.

Even though humour may sometimes be more a consequence rather than a cause of peer status, rejected children may believe that they are ineffective in using humour in peer relations. Unlike many of the neglected, they may feel alone; yet they may lack knowledge about the strategies and purposes of humour in making friends. To cope with threatening situations, they may substitute hostility for humour.

Some rejected children may not be able to gain peer acceptance through physical attractiveness or abilities. The cultivation of a humour reputation is presumably an easier route. It is one that may be influenced by parents and teachers in the light of evidence, from studies in which experimenters have not set aside conversational rules, that children ordinarily are capable of concepts of friendship that go beyond mere physical characteristics.

GENDER CONCEPTS

Children's peer relations are closely connected to their sex-role preferences. They are very concerned about how their appearance and behaviour conforms to sex-role conventions and stereotypes. From at least 2 years of age, they have knowledge of sex-role stereotypes and the appropriateness of games and clothes for boys and girls (Weinraub et al., 1984).

According to Kohlberg (1966; Kohlberg & Ullian, 1974), children's sex-role development is influenced by an understanding of gender concepts. (Another account that focuses on the different treatment boys and girls receive from parents is discussed in the next chapter.) Of special importance is the establishment of a stable concept of gender identity. This concept involves the stable and constant categorisation of the self despite superficial opposite-sex transformations in features such as dress.

Kohlberg, like Selman, was inspired by Piagetian theory and methodology. He contended that, since young children centre on the perceptual appearances rather than the invariant features of a transformation, they base their judgements of gender on changes in games and clothes. Thus the concept of gender identity is derived from conservation abilities. Once children have achieved a stable concept of gender, they know that, for example, a boy will remain a boy even if he wears girls' clothing or plays girls' games. In efforts to live up to a self-definition as a boy or girl, children seek out sex-appropriate activities.

In tests of Kohlberg's account, Slaby and Frey's (1975) gender-constancy interview has been widely used (for example, Ruble, Balaban, & Cooper, 1981; Smetana & Letourneau, 1984). The measure consists of 14 questions and counterquestions: 9 questions on children's knowledge of their "gender identity" (e.g., Are you a girl or boy?), 2 questions on gender stability (e.g., When you were a little baby were you a boy or a girl? When you grow up will you be a mummy or daddy?), and 3 questions on "gender consistency" (e.g., If you wore (opposite sex of subject) clothes would you be a boy or a girl? If you played (opposite sex of the subject) games, would you be a girl or a boy?) The counterquestions were designed to probe the certainty of the children's original responses (i.e., If you played (opposite sex of subject) games, would you be a (opposite sex of subject's first response)?). Children seem to find the identity questions (given first) easier than the stability questions (given second). The consistency questions (given last) are most difficult.

However, support for a relationship between sex-typed behaviour and gender constancy remains inconclusive (Huston, 1983; Martin & Halverson, 1981; 1983). Contrary to the quantity and relevance rules, children may perceive gender-constancy questions to be pointless or have answers that are obvious. Since they do not share the experimenter's purpose to test children's knowledge of gender concepts, their answers might be influenced by the context and order in which the questions are asked. As on conservation tasks, at least some may be switching their responses in an effort to satisfy the experimenter.

In fact, gender constancy has been shown to be closely related to performance on conservation tasks (Marcus & Overton, 1978). The sequence of questions and counterquestions in the gender-constancy interview, while not identical, are very similar in nature and may be perceived as redundant and to violate the quantity rule. In the traditional conservation experiment, post-transformation questions are more difficult to answer than pre-transformation ones, just as questions on gender consistency are more difficult than those on identity and stability. The repetition of items may provoke children, who are uncertain in the first place, to change their answers. Alternatively, when seen from the child's point of view, the questions may seem sillier and sillier and demand even sillier answers. According to this analysis, repetition should result in a lack of gender constancy on the more "difficult" or silly consistency items. If children are given the consistency items first, they should provide more gender-constant responses.

In a study which we carried out (Siegal & Robinson, 1987), the interview questions were posed in a reversed order. We hypothesised that more gender-constant answers would be given when the interview questions were asked in a reversed order than in the usual order. In addition, to supplement the responses on the consistency items with justifications, children were asked to give causal attributions for the presence or absence of gender consistency in the responses of others their own age. If the absence of consistency reflects a willingness to satisfy demand characteristics of the interview, this type of response should produce "external" attributions expressed in terms of a desire to please an adult.

The participants in the study were 30 boys and 30 girls whose ages ranged from 42 to 54 months with a mean of 47.9 months. The children attended kindergartens and preschools located in middle class areas. The experimenter was a female undergraduate student in her early 20s.

The study consisted of two parts in which each child was seen individually. Half the children received one part first (i.e., the gender constancy interview in the traditional or reversed order) and the other part second (i.e., the attribution measures); the sequence was switched for the remainder.

In the first part, the experimenter gave the interview questions in a reversed order to 15 boys and 15 girls. First, she asked the gender-consistency questions on retaining gender while wearing the clothes and playing the games of the opposite sex, together with the counterquestions (although the purpose of counterquestions may remain obscure to young children). Then the gender-stability questions and counterquestions were followed by the gender-identity ones. In the latter case, as in the Slaby and Frey study, dolls and photographs served as props. The remaining children received the gender constancy interview in the traditional order with the questions on identity asked first, stability second, and consistency third. Responses were scored following the criteria used by Slaby and Frey. A child was credited with gender constancy on a question only if both the question and the counterquestion were answered correctly.

In the second part, the experimenter gave the children four stories on gender consistency: two dealt with games and two with clothes. The story characters were the same sex as the subjects and the order of story presentation was counterbalanced across subjects. For one of the stories involving games and one involving clothes, the story character made a gender-constant response; in the others, he or she gave a response that indicated a lack of gender constancy.

After hearing each story, the subjects were asked to attribute the story character's response to an "internal" source (i.e., his or her own beliefs) or to an "external" source (i.e., pretending to please the grown-up questioner). To control for recency effects in the children's attributions, the order of the internal and external alternatives was varied systematically across the stories as shown in parentheses. For example:

Gender constancy present. A grown-up asked a little boy called John who was 4 years old whether he would be a boy or a girl if he wore girls' clothes. John said that he would still be a boy if he wore girls' clothes. Do you think that John really thought that he would still be a boy if he wore girls' clothes or was John just pretending to please the grown-up? (Do you think John was just pretending to please the grown-up, or did John really think that he would still be a boy if he wore girls' clothes?)

Gender constancy absent. A grown-up asked a little girl called Michelle who was 4 years old whether she would be a boy or a girl if she played boys' games. Michelle said that she would be a boy if she played boys' games. Do you think that Michelle was just pretending to please the grown-up, or did Michelle really think that she would be a boy if she played boys' games? (Do you think that Michelle really thought that she would be a boy if she played boys' games, or was Michelle just pretending in order to please the grown-up?)

All of the children were correct on the gender identity and stability interview questions. As predicted, the order in which the questions were asked had a significant effect on the children's responses to gender consistency. Of the 30 children in the reversed order condition, 23 out of 30 (76.7%) gave gender-constant responses on both items involving clothes and games compared to only 10 of the 30 children in the traditional order condition. Far more external attributions were given when the story character was described as lacking gender constancy than when gender constancy was present in the character's responses.

Several limitations of our study should be noted. The age range was rather restricted in comparison to previous work; younger children may not have responded to the interview items in the same way. Additionally, the reversed order procedure may have overestimated knowledge of gender consistency and, in the absence of additional information on the children's sex-role attitudes and behaviours, the possibility of "pseudo-constancy" (correct answers based on some incorrect source) in the children's responses must be recognised. The choice of attribution for the responses of other children in stories can be interpreted to supplement the pattern of responses on the interview items; alternatively, the interview responses may be independent of attributions since it is possible for children to maintain that peers hold genuine or false beliefs in gender consistency (or its absence) irrespective of their own beliefs.

Nevertheless, while these qualifications remain, our hypothesis that the lack of gender constancy shown by children in the traditional interview format is influenced by the context in which the questions are posed was supported. Through prolonged questioning on the topic of gender that can contravene the quantity and relevance rules, at least some children may change their responses in an effort to be silly, cute or attractive instead of correct. This scenario is illustrated in Fig. 5.2.

Gelman and her co-workers (Gelman, Collman, & Maccoby, 1986) have reported a study which strengthens our conclusion that young children often do not rely on perceptual appearances when judging gender. In their

FIG 5.2 An illustration of the possible context of lack of gender constancy.

study, for example, preschoolers were told that boys have "andro" in their blood and girls have "estro" in theirs. Then they were shown pictures that conflicted with these properties, such as a boy who looked like a girl. The preschoolers were asked to infer whether the boy or girl had andro or estro. While they performed poorly on a traditional gender-constancy task, the preschoolers correctly ignored perceptual information in specifying the properties of the children in the pictures. They had less success at using properties like andro to classify gender in perceptually discrepant cases but, as Gelman and her colleagues note, similar difficulties may plague adults.

Although considerable research on children's knowledge about persons has been generated from Piaget's approach, much of this work has consisted of interview studies in which questioners have been inadvertently prone to infringe conversational rules. More recent experiments are attuned to the need to pose questions which are relevant, non-redundant, and which avoid ambiguity. These have illustrated that young children can have meaningful peer relations and concepts of friendship and gender identity.

6 Authority and Academic Skills

The experiments discussed so far have shown that many children at least as young as 4 or 5 years of age are at times often equipped to identify causal relations between objects and to distinguish between appearance and reality. Contrary to the broad Piagetian thesis that young children are egocentric, they have at least some understanding of mental states and false beliefs. They can often report differences between knowing and pretending and have an understanding of friendship and gender identity. To explain differences between these results and those of Piaget and his followers, I have developed the theme that experimenters' departures from conversational rules can account for children's lack of success on many cognitive tasks.

If young children are often able to detect causality, to represent objects and viewpoints, and to understand persons, why do so many ultimately have difficulty in acquiring academic skills at school and, more generally, in following the directions of adults? My hypothesis is that, in part, children have an implicit theory of child care and parental authority which is often not recognised by adults whose own theory of what children know is close to that of Piaget. The beliefs held by adults can serve to weaken the potential quality of parental involvement in promoting academic skills. This involvement may fall short of what children are capable and place obstacles in the way of adult–child communication. For example, should adults believe that children cannot understand simple instructions about a concept, they may decide that to talk to children is a waste of time. In Grice's (1975, p. 49) terminology, they may "opt out" of the Co-operative Principle altogether and express messages such as "I cannot say more; my lips are sealed." To elicit children's compliance, they resort to coercive or rote techniques without a verbal rationale and avoid challenging instruction in academic skills.

However, given that children have a theory of the legitimate uses of adult authority, they often evaluate adults' verbal inputs positively and have poor perceptions of adults' passivity, permissiveness, or coercion. These perceptions, in part, may contribute to non-compliance, with negative consequences for academic progress and concern for others.

Experiments have now cast a favourable light on a conversational involvement which uses reasoning to ensure that children follow directions. It has also been shown that children can and do advance in reading and number skills through an early individualised instruction that takes care to build upon their capabilities. In the light of the evidence which undermines the idea of a basic conceptual limitation in early childhood, consideration must be given to parent–child relations and their effect on success at school.

KNOWLEDGE OF RATIONALES

A central aspect of children's development is learning to follow adult instructions and standards for behaviour in the absence of external surveillance. Should they be unable to understand the rationale underlying directions in conversation, parents might feel warranted in using other, more coercive tactics to ensure that children complete a task or behave with concern for others. In exasperation, some parents may decide that their involvement is not worthwhile at all. To what extent, then, can children understand the rationales underlying adults' behaviours?

In his discussion of causal attribution, Kelley (1973) noted cases in which adults may regard multiple causes as sufficient to produce behaviour. When both intrinsic (voluntary) and extrinsic (external) causes are present, they can use a "discounting" strategy in recognising that external factors can pressure an individual to behave against his or her will. In explaining this behaviour, they may discount and assign less weight to the causal importance of intrinsic causes compared to cases in which only intrinsic causes are present.

Can young children use this strategy? Piaget (1932) would suggest that they do not. He proposed that they do not distinguish between different sorts of transgressions and have a unilateral respect for adult authority. They believe that the consequences of an act should determine the degree of naughtiness and punishment irrespective of the perpetrator's intentions. As described in Chapter Three, according to Piaget, children also believe that mishaps can result in immanent justice. They think that adults are so powerful that misfortune such as illness will inevitably befall those who are disobedient.

Researchers applying Kelley's ideas to children have sought to demonstrate, on the basis of Piaget's position, that they cannot use a discounting strategy in reasoning about the causes of behaviour and that they do not discriminate between a voluntary and forced compliance to an adult request. For example, Karniol and Ross (1976) asked children and adults to judge characters in stories presented in pairs. In one story, a child would play with a particular toy without any (extrinsic) suggestions from an adult. In the other, the child would play with a toy following an adult directive to do so. The task was to say which child really wanted to play with the toy. In contrast to older children and adults, kindergarten children showed no clear preference for one child over the other.

Some years ago, it could be speculated that children's responses in this sort of study might be influenced by methodological problems, including difficulties related to the story content and the desire to give acceptable answers to the experimenter (Siegal, 1982, pp. 114–116). More recently, the results of two studies have challenged the conclusion that young children do not use a discounting strategy.

First, Dalenberg, Bierman, and Furman (1984) presented children in kindergarten, second grade and fourth grade with stories in which a boy engaged in an activity (e.g., playing with a puzzle, going to bed early) in the absence or presence of a reward (50 cents or a cookie). For example, "Here is Steve. Steve's mom tells him that if he plays with the puzzle, she will give him a cookie." Steve plays with the puzzle. Steve's mom gives him a cookie. The children indicated how well the story characters such as Steve like the activity by pointing to one of a series of seven faces that ranged in expression from a large frown (point 1 on a 1 to 7 scale) to a large smile (point 7). They did this in one of two experimental conditions: "reward-contamination" and "reward-free". In the reward-contamination condition, an experimenter asked the children, "How much does (the story character) like to (do the activity) in the story? Why did (the story character) do the activity in the story?" In the reward-free condition, the experimenter said, "Now it is a whole week later. Steve is alone. His mom is home. Steve can decide to (do the activity) or not to (do the activity). What will he decide? How much does he like (doing the activity)?" The children predicted what the story character would do, one week later, in the absence of a reward.

Kindergarten children in the reward-contamination condition did not clearly use a discounting strategy. But Dalenberg and her colleagues reinterpreted this result to be due to their liking of the reward rather than to an inability to attribute accurately the cause of a story character's compliance. In the reward-contamination condition, the youngest children may have simply seized upon "liking" as the most salient explanation for compliance; in contrast, those in the reward-free condition differentiated between the constrained story character who earlier performed the activity under extrinsic constraints and the character who performed voluntarily in the absence of sanctions. They rated the constrained character as less likely to want to do the activity.

Second, Dix and Grusec (1983) carried out an examination of causal attributions for the helping of story characters. The participants were at four age levels: 5 to 6 years, 8 to 9 years, 11 to 13 years and adults who were parents of children aged 5 to 13. Each one heard six stories representing different strategies used by parents to elicit helping behaviour on the part of children: power assertion (threats of punishment with or without reasoning); modelling (with or without reasoning); and spontaneous helping (with or without reasoning). For example:

One day, Mom, Carolyn, and little Mike were putting on their winter clothes. They were going to play in the snow. Little Mike couldn't get his boots on. He got mad and said, "I can't do it." Mom said, "It's alright, Mike. Those boots are hard to put on, especially for someone as small as you. You just need help (reasoning statement). I'll help you. Stick your leg out straight. I'll try to pull your boot up." A moment later little Mike was having trouble with the other boot. Carolyn did what Mom did before. Carolyn said, "Here, Mike, let me help you. You hold your leg straight. I'll pull your boot." (Modelling.)

For each story, the subjects were asked to indicate whether Carolyn (and the other central story characters) helped willingly or to conform with the wishes of an adult. Therefore, either an internal or external causal attribution could be given. In response to the stories, even 5- and 6-year-olds discriminated between causes attributable to different parental strategies. They gave external attribution for power assertion and internal attributions for modelling and spontaneous helping.

The subjects in Dix and Grusec's study were also asked to infer personality traits by rating how helpful the central story character would be usually. Unlike the older children and adults, the 5- and 6-year-olds did not discriminate among the characters in the different conditions. A character who complied under power assertion was rated as helpful a person as one who had modelled helping spontaneously. Yet, as shown in the Dalenberg study, young children did use a discounting strategy when the question clearly referred to a character with a history of compliance. Without knowledge of this history, Dix and Grusec's children may have misinterpreted the request to give "trait inferences" for each of the story characters as a form of repeated questioning. To infer helpfulness in an individual's personality is similar to perceiving the cause of helping. Having answered the first of the experimenter's questions by attributing causality to a story character's actions, children may expect that they should change their answer on a second question that is very similar.

CHILDREN'S THEORY OF LEGITIMATE ADULT AUTHORITY

Thus, consistent with the research on the understanding of physical causality discussed in Chapter Three, young children have at least some capacity to understand the rationales underlying adults' instructions. They can use a discounting strategy to distinguish between a compliance that is intrinsically, rather than extrinsically, motivated. Can they go a step further? Can they distinguish between behaviour that ought to be regulated by authority as opposed to that which ought to be left to a child's own devices?

Recall that many preschoolers are able to distinguish between social and moral transgressions. They evaluate the punishment due to social transgressions as tied to specific contexts whereas they view moral transgressions to be naughty and worthy of punishment regardless of context. According to Weston and Turiel (1980) and Tisak (1986), children advocate that the use of adult authority should be limited to prohibit violations of moral transgressions. It should not be used to interfere in situations concerning social transgressions or personal choices that do not necessarily affect others' welfare.

Weston and Turiel presented four hypothetical situations to a group of children aged 4 to 11 years. Each situation contrasted schools in which the given act was permitted or prohibited by school policy. The situations were: (1) a child removes his or her clothes on the school playground after getting too warm from playing; (2) a child hits and pushes another child out of a swing after discovering that all the swings on the playground are occupied; (3) a child goes outside to play, leaving some toys on the floor after playing with them; and (4) a child refuses to share his or her snack with another child visiting the school who asked for some crackers because there were none remaining in the box.

Within a particular school setting, the children were asked to evaluate the policies and the behaviour of the culprit in the situation. They also predicted and evaluated the intervention (or non-intervention) of a teacher in the context of different school policies.

Regardless of age, children generally felt that a teacher would reprimand a child who hit another even in a school where hitting did not contravene policy. They viewed a permissive school policy positively in the cases of undressing, leaving toys on the floor, and refusing to share but they evaluated negatively a policy that permitted hitting. However, young children responded that the action of a child who hit in a permissive school was all right while the older children said that hitting was wrong.

To interpret this finding, Weston and Turiel referred to age-related differences in causal attributions. They suggested that, until the age of 8 or 9 years, children view extrinsic situational factors to be the main constraints on behaviour. Therefore they do not negatively evaluate the behaviour of a child when that behaviour is permitted by school policy. However, given the results reported by Dalenberg, Dix, and their colleagues, Weston and Turiel may be underestimating the capacity of younger children to infer the causes of behaviour. Indeed, young children may be more likely than older ones to respond in a desirable fashion when questioned by an adult about a child who acted within the bounds of school rules. In any event, there were no age differences in predictions of teachers' behaviour.

A more recent study by Tisak (1986) supports young children's ability to delimit the bounds of authority. The method was quite similar to that of Weston and Turiel except that it dealt with conceptions of parental authority rather than teachers' authority in schools. Children aged 6 to 11 years were given hypothetical situations with 3 themes: (1) taking another child's toy (stealing); (2) leaving dishes on the table after eating (family chores); and (3) playing with a forbidden friend. In each instance, they were asked whether there should be an obligation to follow the instructions of a parental authority and whether a child should respond to another child's transgression in the absence of an explicit requirement to do so. Even the youngest children drew boundaries around the jurisdiction of parents. For example, they indicated a stronger likelihood of responding to another's transgression in the case of stealing than in the cases of neglecting chores and, especially, choosing prohibited friends. Children of all ages maintained the greater legitimacy of parental rule-making for stealing than for regulating chores or choosing friends.

Therefore, children do distinguish between the gravity of different types of transgressions and there are areas in which they prefer that behaviour should be left unregulated such as dress, hairstyles, friendship choices, and toy preferences. Even preschoolers can often identify acts that are voluntary and those that are constrained by extrinsic forces.

What then are the consequences of children's perceptions of parental control for their voluntary acceptance of adults' instructions? We might surmise that methods to elicit compliance should aim to promote internal attributions. The more subtle the methods of persuasion, the less they will attribute their behaviour to extrinsic forces. Reasoning should be more effective than techniques which assert the power of the parent.

However, considerable controversy exists over the role of the parent. For attribution theorists (see for example, Lepper, 1983; Lepper & Gilovich, 1981; Lewis, 1981), children's following of instructions in the absence of external surveillance is promoted by the least and most subtle pressure that is sufficient to obtain compliance. Alternatively, for researchers such as Baumrind (1983), "salient" techniques of "firm control" are most effective, and these often must be moderately severe to be effective.

Both positions converge, though, to emphasise the importance of children's perceptions and evaluations of authority. As an advocate of an attributional approach, Lewis (1981, p. 562) has suggested that from the child's point of view "rules may not be imposed or enforced at all but distilled from the child's own social interactions". Children's sense of voluntary compliance—their "internalisation" of adult standards for behaviour—may be essential in following directions. To support the use of parental firm control, Baumrind (1983, p. 141) has maintained: ". . . the use of reasoning accompanied by power-assertion should be more effective with young children than reasoning alone: with young children a display of power captures their attention and clarifies in their minds that compliance is required, whereas the use of reason without a display of power often signals to the child that the parent is indecisive about requiring compliance."

Neither Lewis nor Baumrind deal specifically with differences in the socialisation roles of the mother and father. Often they group both together in referring to parents. All the same, our work suggests that differences in the treatment of sons and daughters by mothers and fathers can provide an explanation for differences in children's perceptions of parental control techniques and resulting compliance.

In one study (Siegal & Cowen, 1984), we gave children in preschool to Grade 12 stories where a child disobeyed a mother, including cases of simple disobedience and physical or psychological harm to others (for example, laughing at a crippled person who crosses a road and skipping inside a room causing a lamp to fall and break). An experimenter read each story and listed the child-rearing techniques used by four mothers. She asked the children to consider each mother in turn and told them to indicate how right each of the mothers was to do as she did. The techniques fell into the broad categories defined by Hoffman (1970): (1) induction in which the mother was described to the subjects as reasoning with the culprit and pointing out the harmful consequences of the transgression for the self and others; (2) power assertion in which she was described as physically punishing the culprit (a salient method of control); and (3) love withdrawal in which she was described as telling the culprit that she would not have anything more to do with the child for the time being. In addition, a fourth type of mother was described as choosing not to intervene, believing that the child would learn independently. The inclusion of permissiveness as a discipline technique allowed comparisons to be made between evaluations of non-intervention and different forms of intervention. At all ages, children generally expressed strong approval for induction backed by milder approval for physical punishment. The nature of the situation was a strong influence on their evaluations, with children appreciating the mother's flexibility.

Yet in a follow-up study on evaluations of fathers' behaviours using the same methodology and similar age groups (Siegal & Barclay, 1985), young children aged 5 and 6 years showed no clear preferences for the same techniques as used by fathers, and their ratings of fathers were not strongly determined by the situation. Physical punishment often received approval compared to induction. Moreover, in contrast to the study of perceptions of mothers, boys and girls differed in their ratings. Boys in general rated fathers more favourably than did girls, particularly in their use of physical punishment in situations of simple disobedience and physical harm to the self. Girls rated fathers' use of induction more highly than boys in the simple disobedience situation.

A qualification to these studies is that the children were asked to consider hypothetical rather than real parents. However, the results fit well with the observations of Lynn (1959; 1962) and Block (1983) that, compared to the father, the mother is generally more visible in child rearing. Since mothers ordinarily have a greater day-to-day involvement with children, they are likely to be seen by both boys and girls as more sensitive than fathers to individual situations. Girls are provided with a model for sex-appropriate behaviour which boys lack, and they may be more likely to advocate the use of induction and to reject the use of physical punishment. Girls' willingness to follow adults' directions may be promoted by their self-perceptions of gentleness and physical weakness (Ullian, 1984) and by mothers' frequent mention of states of feeling in conversations with daughters at an early age (Dunn, Bretherton, & Munn, 1987). Fathers, by contrast, are comparatively unavailable as sources of induction and sensitivity. The boy is left more on his own to search for the appropriate model.

In the absence of the extensive day-to-day interaction that marks the mother–child relationship, father–child evaluations may be more likely to be influenced by mutual sex-typing. Boys' and girls' differential evaluations of the father's behaviour are consistent with his different treatment of boys and girls. In their review of the research on sex differences, Maccoby and Jacklin (1974, p. 348) report that they were handicapped by a lack of information on the father. But in agreement with the differential socialisation theory of Johnson (1963; 1975), they speculated that "fathers may differentiate between the sexes to a much greater degree than mothers". Since then considerable research has indicated that fathers, more than mothers, do differentiate between boys and girls (e.g., Bronstein, 1984; Langlois & Downs, 1980; Tauber, 1979). While some studies have used multiple measures of parent–child interaction and often only a few of these have revealed differences related to the sex of the parent, results that are significant provide general support for a pattern of differential behaviour that is specific to the father (Siegal, 1987). In particular, the father gives more positive and negative reinforcement to boys than girls, is more punitive, and uses more firm control techniques. Though there are studies in which no differences at all have been found in parents' treatment of boys and girls, differences restricted specifically to the mother have been virtually non-existent.

For girls, given the greater day-to-day involvement of the mother, a harmonious, peaceful environment in which subtle control can be used may often be effective in promoting an acceptance of adults' instructions. But for boys, the affective atmosphere of the home may preclude the use of subtle control. Owing to the father's and son's orientations towards the use of power assertion and the father's differential treatment, the boy may respond more positively to a parental authority that is made salient through firm discipline techniques. To achieve self-control, the boy may seek to bring himself in line with environmental forces. He may associate and identify vicariously with powerful others such as the father (see Rothbaum, Weisz, & Snyder, 1982, pp. 20–21). With greater paternal involvement and a father–son relation as close as that which ordinarily exists between the mother and daughter, subtle control techniques may be effective and appropriate for sons as well. In this respect, fathers may opt into the Co-operative Principle and initiate conversations with sons about feelings and rationales for following directions.

To promote academic skills and concern for others, parents may use subtle techniques that avoid power assertion. In his many writings, Sigel (1981; see also Johnson & McGillicuddy-Delisi, 1983) has called for parents to use "distancing behaviours" to encourage learning in children. These are behaviours that place demands on the child to separate himself or herself by representations in space and time from the ongoing field of observable events. The child is required to "anticipate outcomes, recall events, and attend to transformations of objects or phenomena". Through high-distancing strategies, parents can lead the child to gain insight into the mental states of others. Opportunities are provided to plan and to evaluate the consequences of actions.

Once children are at school, their perceptions of the quality of this parental involvement can provide a basis for an intrinsic motivation to do well on academic subjects. Grolnick and Ryan (1986) interviewed mothers and fathers of 48 children in Grades 3 to 6 in a rural elementary school in upstate New York to identify a group of "autonomy-promoting" parents (particularly mothers) who used reasoning and empathy in setting limits. These parents were more likely to have children who were judged by their teachers to be successful at school. Compared to children of parents who used power assertive techniques such as physical punishment, children of autonomy-promoting parents were rated as displaying fewer learning difficulties and behaviour problems. Grolnick and Ryan suggest that parental support for autonomy promoted children's acceptance of classroom rules.

Besides the use of autonomy-promoting techniques of control, parents' attitudes and beliefs about development may influence children. A parent who has accurate expectations about children's capabilities may be best equipped to promote not only their compliance and responsiveness to others' interests and feelings but their success at school.

PARENTAL INVOLVEMENT

One of the most important aims for children is to instil an intrinsic motivation to pursue reading, mathematics, and other school subjects voluntarily. Miller (1986) sought to test the hypothesis that the mother's knowledge of the child enables her to create an "optimally challenging environment". First graders were given either traditional Piagetian measures (such as conservation of number and length) or items from the Stanford-Binet test of intelligence (such as naming five days of the week). Their mothers were shown these tasks and were asked questions about the probable responses, both for their own child and for children in general. Mothers more commonly overestimated than underestimated their children's performance. The most accurate mothers had the most successful children. While these mothers may have provided the most stimulating environments, it may be the case that all mothers are optimistic in praising their children's performance so that mothers who happen to have an intelligent child will be scored as more accurate than those who do not.

The extensive work of Stevenson and his colleagues (Stevenson, Lee, & Stigler, 1986; see also Uttal, Lummis, & Stevenson, 1988) is compatible with the interpretation of unjustified optimism among mothers of children who are not high achievers. They carried out a comparison of the factors underlying the mathematics achievement of American, Taiwanese, and Japanese school children from Minneapolis, Taipei, and Sendai. The cognitive abilities of the three groups appeared to be similar in the early primary school years. Yet by Grade 5, the Japanese and Taiwanese far outstripped the Americans in mathematics. Parents in Japan and Taiwan indicated a greater concern with homework. For example, the percentage of parents who bought their fifth graders workbooks in mathematics was 58% in Japan, 56% in Taiwan, but only 28% in the United States. Only 63% of the American fifth graders had desks at home compared to 98% of the Japanese and 95% of the Taiwanese.

But despite the superiority of their children's performance at mathematics, Japanese and Taiwanese parents often expressed dissatisfaction with the quality of education received by the children. By contrast, the

American parents were often very satisfied and could even be termed to have an attitude of complacency and overoptimism. While Japanese and, to a lesser extent, Taiwanese parents focused on effort as a factor contributing to academic success, American parents were more likely to rate ability as a key factor. The belief in success through hard work was more apparent in Japan and Taiwan. Western commentators often mention the stressful nature of the Japanese education system with a serious, intense emphasis on the importance of academic success. Even so, the Stevenson study found no cross-cultural differences in the children's ratings of happiness at school. They conclude by advocating an increased involvement in reading, mathematics, and other elementary school subjects by American parents.

In a very important though speculative article, Stanovich (1986) has attempted to explain the acquisition of literacy in terms of "Matthew effects". He maintains that the process of learning to read can be viewed in terms of effects in which the rich get richer and the poor get poorer. He paints a scenario in which children's knowledge of the alphabet and their ability to "decode" correspondences between letters and sounds leads to successful reading experiences. Increased vocabulary in turn leads to children's acquisition of a vocabulary of words that can be read which in turn produces further successful reading experiences and fluency in comprehension.

The outcome is a series of bidirectional or reciprocal effects in which success at reading skills and reading experience are mutual determinants of each other. Children's reading experience can lead to an association with literate peers that in turn increases vocabulary and comprehension. Stanovich has argued that young children who have difficulty in distinguishing sounds and in matching sounds to letters will later become more and more disadvantaged compared to children who have performed well on these ground floor prerequisites for reading. He calls for a "surgical strike" around the preschool period to diagnose and remediate reading problems.

Although the notion of Matthew effects may seem appealing as a framework for efforts at intervention, the precise nature of bidirectional forces in literacy in exceedingly difficult to locate. Let us consider a somewhat different scenario. In a disordered home environment, parents do not equip children with a knowledge of moral and social transgressions. Their behaviour leads to rejection by literate and numerate peers and poor motivation and concentration at school. Their poor academic performance in turn leads to a further lack of acceptance by peers who do well. In New Zealand longitudinal study of boys' reading skills (McGee, Williams, Share, Anderson, & Silva, 1986), a strong association was found between reading disability and behaviour problems. One interpretation was that reading disability exacerbates problem behaviour that already exists at school entry. Coie and Krehbiel (1984) have suggested that behaviour problems may be reduced by involving children on tasks that enhance the acquisition of basic reading and writing skills. The ground floor in acquiring literacy is still during the early childhood period; but it calls for a broader form of intervention that enlists the home environment, and individual attention from the adult, as a context conducive to transmitting academic skills. There are now a variety of studies on instructing children in this manner.

INDIVIDUALISED INSTRUCTION IN READING AND NUMBER: SOME EXAMPLES

Hewison and Tizard (1980) showed how children's reading can benefit from an increased parental involvement. They examined home background factors and reading ability and found a strong relationship between mothers' self-reports of hearing the child read (referred to as "coaching") and reading achievement in 7- and 8-year-olds. In a sample of 70 British children with average IQ test scores, 24 of the 32 good readers studied by Hewison and Tizard had coaching mothers as opposed to only 8 of 38 poor readers.

Hearing children read can involve training and language skills. Work by Bryant and Bradley (1983), also in Britain, and by Content, Kolinsky, Morais, and Bertelson (1986) in Belgium has shown how 4- and 5-year-olds can be trained to have an awareness of language in matching sounds to letters. The children seen by Bryant and Bradley later performed well on standardised reading tests compared to others who did not receive this training in early childhood. Furthermore, Goswami (1986) has reported that children who are learning to read can often be prompted to use analogies in "decoding" new words. For example, they can use the word "beak" to read, "peak", and "rail" to read "pail".

Young children's representation abilities can also be used to promote links between what they already know and the symbols and regularities they are expected to acquire. As the following three examples illustrate, instructing children to use forms of representation may be a means to draw out their implicit knowledge about number. First, Fuson (1986a; 1986b) has reported that the learning of addition and subtraction can be facilitated by "counting-on" strategies in which children's attention is drawn to finger patterns as a form of representing sums and differences. Second, Resnick and Ford (1981, pp. 210–213) have described how symbols may assist school-aged children to add and subtract using rows of blocks arranged in "tens" and "units" columns. For example, to subtract 47 from 85, the 85 is first represented as 8 ten-bars in the tens column and 5 ones-cubes in the units column. To arrive at the correct answer (38), the experimenter induces the child to notice that there are not enough ones-cubes in the units column to remove 7. The child is then trained to "borrow" a ten-bar from the tens column to the units column, separate the bar into ones-cubes, remove 7 of the cubes as part of subtracting 47, write down the remaining number of cubes in the units column, then remove four more ten-bars from the tens column and count and write down the number of bars remaining to complete the problem. Third, Hudson (1983) has shown that 4- and 5-year-olds can solve subtraction tasks that involve comparisons between sets using pretend items such as birds and worms, dogs and bones, butterflies and objects. If shown five birds and two worms and asked how many birds won't get a worm, children will respond with the correct answer.

To instruct children on number problems often involves the need to invoke a relevant context. But more than relevance is required to draw out a mathematical understanding. Wood (1988, p. 199) points out, some examples provided to children in the name of relevance may actually make number tasks more difficult. They may be asked, for example, "If it takes three men two days to dig a hole, how long would it take two men to dig the same hole?" This type of question may elicit imagery from everyday life and prompt responses such as "Have they got different tools?"

In this regard, Cummins, Kintsch, Reusser, and Weimer (1988) have proposed that, rather than the absence of a capacity for representation, primary schoolers' difficulties with "word arithmetic problems" can be attributed to their misunderstanding of the uses of words such as "some" and linguistic forms such as "How many more Xs than Ys?" and "How many Xs do they have altogether?" It has been argued (Willis & Fuson, 1988) that such difficulties can be approached through having children (for example, second graders) use schematic drawings to represent the various types of addition and subtraction problems: operations involving comparisons between quantities, changes to quantities resulting in a story character possessing more or less, and putting together quantities possessed by story characters. For example, a large box can be placed over two small boxes containing the numbers possessed by two characters to represent and clarify the meaning of a "put-together" problem.

A further illustration of how difficulties in word meaning can explain performance on number problems comes from some initial work on children's representation of fractions (Siegal, 1989). For many young children, their theory of number seems limited to natural counting numbers that are used in ordinary conversation. Yet to understand zero and fractions, they must accommodate their theory of number to accept zero as a "non-count" number and fractions as those which fill in the gaps between the "natural" counting numbers that are ordinarily used in conversation. My purpose in this experiment was to determine whether difficulties at understanding zero and fractions can be addressed through clarifying the requirements of number tasks.

The participants were 20 first graders (mean age in years and months = 6-4, range 6-0 to 6-9) and 20 second graders (mean age = 7-3, range 6-10 to 7-10). The children were tested individually and first asked to order numbers on five cards from smallest to largest: 0, 1, 2, 3. They were asked to do the same with the cards 0, 1/4, 1/3, 1/2, and 1. While of course the children could order the whole numbers, no first graders and only two of the second graders could order the fractions. Most sorted by ignoring the inversion sign ("/"): 0, 1, 1/2, 1/3, 1/4.

They were then shown a "/" sign, told it means "out of" and given the examples 1/2, 1/3, 1/4 on cards matched with pictures of parts and whole cakes. The children were directed to place cards representing fractions of the cakes in between cards representing 0 and 1 cakes and to place a card representing the appropriate fraction under each cake.

The following three phases consisted of: (1) matching fractions and whole numbers to a representation; (2) comparing fractions and whole numbers in an everyday context; and (3) transferring knowledge about fractions to numbers such as 1/20. For example, in the first phase, the children were shown a Lego boy (or girl for girls in the experiment) who wanted a drink of juice but was described as ill with a sore throat and unable to talk. They were given two cards, representing one whole glass and a half of a glass, and were told that the boy wanted "this much" (1/2) to drink. The children's task was to select the appropriate card from a row of number cards (0, 1/4, 1/3, 1/2, 1, 2, 3, 4) in order to indicate how much juice the boy wanted and how much he would have wanted had he chosen the other glass. In the second phase, the children were told about twins and triplets who consumed different amounts of food (for example, one twin who ate "this much" (1/4) and the other who ate "that much" (1) with the numbers shown on cards). They were asked to point to the card to indicate who is still hungry compared to the other(s). In the third phase, all the materials were removed and the children were given a fresh set of 12 cards to order by number from the smallest to largest. These consisted of drawings of children who each held up a sign to show the quantity of chocolate bars they had eaten. The numbers were 0, 1/20, 1/10, 1/8, 1/7, 1/6, 1/4, 1/3, 1/2, 1, 2, and 3.

Although fractions are not formally taught until fourth grade, many second graders shared the experimenter's meaning of number to include zero and fractions. For example, 15 out of 20 in the first phase identified the 1/2 card as the amount wanted by the Lego boy. Only three chose a whole number (1 or 3) while one child chose 1/4 and another 1/3. When told that the Lego boy had drunk part of the juice and left some for later, 12 children chose 1/4 to match the representation and 5 chose 1/3. Only two children chose 1/2 and one a whole number (2). Performance of the first graders in this phase was similar with 16 out of 20 identifying the 1/2 card as the amount wanted by the Lego boy. Only two chose a whole number (2 or 4) while one child again chose 1/4 and another 1/3. When told the Lego boy had drunk part of the juice and left some for later, nine children chose 1/4 to match the representation, five chose 1/3, and two chose the whole number 1. One each chose the numbers 1/2, 0, 2, and 4.

In the other phases, there was a disparity between the two age groups. In the second phase, for example, 10 first graders and 14 second graders chose the twin who ate 1/4 of a chocolate bar as still hungry compared to a twin who ate one bar. Performance on the third phase is shown in Table 6.1. Only three first graders sorted the 12 cards correctly compared to the ten second graders who sorted correctly and the two who sorted with minor errors (i.e., 0, 1/7, 1/20, 1/10, 1/8, 1/6, 1/4, 1/3, 1/2, 1, 2, 3; 0, 1/20, 1/10, 1/8, 1/6, 1/7, 1/2, 1/3, 1/4, 1, 2, 3). Three first graders and one second grader failed to transfer a knowledge of inversion to numbers below 1/4. For example, they sorted as follows: 0, 1/4, 1/3, 1/2, 1/6, 1/7, 1/8, 1/10, 1/20, 1, 2, 3. Three second graders placed fractions correctly between 0 and 1 but in the reversed order: for example, 0, 1/2, 1/3, 1/4, 1/6, 1/7, 1/8, 1/10, 1/20, 1, 2, 3. Interestingly, three other children (two first graders and one second grader) sorted the fractions in the correct order after 0 but reversed the order of the whole numbers: 0, 1/20, 1/10, 1/8, 1/7, 1/6, 1/4, 1/3, 1/2, 3, 2, 1. The remaining children ignored the inversion sign and sorted the fractions as if they were whole numbers.

This experiment suggests that children, despite training, interpret fractions as integers. To be sure, there are second graders who do appear to benefit and display some knowledge in advance of the formal instruction that is recieved on fractions in Grade 4. But the largely incorrect pattern

TABLE 6.1
Distribution of Sorting Responses in the Third Phase of the Experiment on Fractions (From Siegal, 1989)

Response	Group	
	First Graders	Second Graders
Sort correctly	3	10
Sort with minor errors	0	2
Reversal of fractions between 0–1	0	3
Reversal of whole numbers (3, 2, 1)	2	1
Failure to transfer	3	1
Inverse sign ignored	12	3
Total numbers of children	20	20

of responses provided by many children in both Grades 1 and 2 may reflect an early theory of number that points to a conceptual problem or limitation in cognitive development.

However, an alternative interpretation exists. For many children, at least part of the difficulty in representing fractions as numbers is the unfamiliar nature of language. This difficulty may be overcome through instruction that stimulates children to relinquish a "whole number" theory. If, as the German philosopher Gottlob Frege (1884/1953, p. 67) maintained, the "content of a statement about number is an assertion about a concept", we must search for content in which the sense of the meaning of number-words such as one-half and one-fourth can be precisely fixed and shared.

In examining children's understanding of fractions, it can be observed that proper names designate live identities which are atomic and indivisible. In learning language, children rarely if ever, use a proper name incorrectly to identify more than one individual (Macnamara, 1982; 1986). While integers can be used to count these identities, fractions cannot. One cannot ordinarily have 1½ Michaels or 2½ boys.

Common names designate continua such as shapes, time, distance, food, and other substances. While we may use fractions to identify continua, often we can get by with integers. A cake or chocolate shaped as a circle and one shaped as a semi-circle may be counted as 1½ but also 2. Thus not only are fractions inapplicable in referring to live identities but fractions may often be pragmatically avoided in the measurement of many continua without losing the sense of a conversation. Without an awareness of the sense of the meaning of fractions, children may fall back on the use of counting principles involving the conventional integers 1, 2, 3, 4, 5 that are generally grasped by the age of 5 years (Gelman & Gallistel, 1978).

Consequently, to ask children how many are a whole circle and a semi-circle involves testing whether they share the presupposition of a number concept that is to be expressed as a fraction. A difficulty in this instance is that circles are cultural artefacts. If children use whole numbers such as "2" to express what the experimenter intends to be a fractional representation (e.g., 1½), it may be tempting to conclude that they do not have the ability to represent fractions. Alternatively, they may have misinterpreted the purpose and context in which the question is asked. They may not be aware that adults conventionally use the shape of a circle to refer to parts and wholes. Frege (1960, p. 83) gives the example, "How many is Great Britain and Ireland?" to illustrate the potency of context. Such questions cannot be answered unless the listener shares the presuppositions implicit in the speaker's request.

For children to understand statements about fractions as assertions about number (and accept 1½ instead of 2 as a description of a circle and semi-circle), contexts are needed in which there is a clear sense of the kind of judgement that needs to be fixed to a continuum. As in experiments on children's knowledge of contamination and the distinction between appearance and reality, food is a familiar context for early mental representation. In fact, it may be the most salient vehicle for the development of category formation in young children (Rozin, 1990). In food preparation, identities such as fish are transformed into continua. As seen in Chapter Three, young children are quite sensitive to the characteristics of animate and non-animate things. Even when no longer alive, fish are natural kinds that retain distinctive physical identity in contrast to their transformed shape as food continua. A whole fish with head and tail intact and a tail of a fish together demand a fractional representation of 1½ in a sense unlike shapes of pies and cakes. Therefore, it should be possible to use food such as fish as a context for drawing out a mathematical understanding of fractions and integers in young children.

Research in this area is presently underway in a series of experiments with first and second graders. Following Lampert's (1986) procedures, the experimenter explains the use of fractions with regard to a series of pictorial representations of identities such as fish having heads and tails and positioned upright. Using paper puzzles and cutouts, the children are shown how fish can be divided into different size parts such as halves, quarter, thirds, fourths, fifths, and sixths, and one-and-a-half. They are required to put together the parts to demonstrate, by manipulating parts of the fish, how different combinations of fractions equal "1" (i.e., four-fourths, three-thirds, two-halves, and two-quarters plus one-half) and are asked to use these representations to solve problems such as ½ + ¼. This is a long-term project and it is early days for results. But based on other number research, it is entirely possible that young children can be instructed to use early symbolic principles of mathematics in this way.

AUTHORITY AS COMPLACENCY?

This brief description illustrates how parental involvement in early individualised instruction could play a key role in the development of literacy and numeracy. Interestingly, of all the subjects taught in school, mathematics is least dependent on the understanding of natural language. Even so, a focus by parents in one-to-one situations can capitalise on children's capacity for representation to clarify the meaning and purpose of language required to succeed on number tasks.

However, guidance is hardly provided by an authority that amounts to complacency. While much more remains to be known about the consequences of parents' attitudes and beliefs for children (for an exposition of possible implications, see Goodnow, 1988; Miller, 1988), the persistence of a complacent ideology demands a re-examination of the issue of education for young children. There are those who worry that demonstrations of the early benefits of teaching will result in formal schooling for 4-year-olds, depriving children of a time for childhood (Zigler, 1987). Yet there is no reason why instruction cannot be imparted informally to children within a warm, enjoyable family atmosphere. At 4 years, an austere formal schooling environment would hardly seem necessary—only a commitment by parents and preschool and daycare workers. As it stands now, in many cases, our underestimation of what parents can do in early childhood may be accompanied by an overestimation of what schools are doing, and will do, to meet children's needs.

It is notable that Piaget's theory is an ideal handmaiden to this complacent approach. At times, his disinterest in applying developmental psychology to education surfaced in statements such as "it is impossible to deduce good pedagogy from psychology" and "it is better for a child to find and invent his own solutions rather than being taught" (L. Smith, 1985, p. 183). As Resnick and Ford (1981, p. 189) have exclaimed, the conception of matching instruction to the children's readiness as shown by their performance on Piagetian tasks is "virtually a counsel of despair for education, because it implies that there is little for teachers to do except to await certain developments". In this regard, we may recall Piaget's uncomplimentary reference to the American dilemma over the means to accelerate development. A more optimistic neo-Piagetian interpretation of "matching" is to give children problems that are moderately challenging for their present capability but are not so difficult as to be incomprehensible. Still, educators have often used Piaget to derive guidelines for schooling on the basis of a notion of developmental readiness. For example, it has been stated that, before children attain the age at which they attend primary school, they "lack a firm foundation of judgement or reasoning". As a consequence, before teaching academic skills such as reading, they should have achieved "readiness" and "prerequisite skills" (Furth & Wachs, 1974, pp. 42–43). The interpretation of Piaget's negative message for education flies in the face of the accumulating wealth of evidence on young children's capacity for understanding and the effectiveness of instruction during the preschool and early primary school years.

7 Models of Knowledge

CONVERSATIONAL RULES FOR KNOWING CHILDREN

Much of the knowledge of children which appears in textbooks on child development has been derived from their responses in interviews with adults. Nevertheless, interviews often involve prolonged or other forms of unconventional questioning methods where children can perceive that conversational rules have been violated. Not enough recognition has been accorded to the shortcomings of these types of studies. Instead of a conceptual limitation, their incorrect responses may reflect uncertainty, a misinterpretation of the meaning or purpose of the question, a desire to give attention-seeking answers, or simply a wish to end the conversation.

We must remember that children are speaking to interrogators who are physically much larger and more powerful and that conversations between children (usually 3 to 4 feet high) and adults (usually 5 to 6 feet high) reflect differences in stature. The ratio is similar to that between average-sized adults and 8-foot giants. Even adult speakers are influenced by the physical characteristics of their listeners. With a more limited experience of the social world and personalities of adults, children may be highly suggestible in an interview setting. They may fear the unsuspecting adult who nevertheless approaches the interview with gentleness and sincerity.

Moreover, children recognise that adults ordinarily have more knowledge than they do. As Freeman, Sinha, and Condliffe (1981) have pointed out, this recognition adds to the imbalance of power that is implicit in conversations between children and adults. If knowledge creates power, a situation of confrontation may develop in which the children can feel obliged by using extraneous information provided by adults to give a response. The result may be an answer to a question different from the one that the experimenter had intended.

The power relations in conversations between adults and children are like the relations between powerful and submissive groups of adults. For example, anthropologists and linguists have observed differences in the conversations of white and Aboriginal Australians (Eades, 1982). They have found considerable "gratuitous concurrence" among Aborigines who attempt to accommodate to the requests of white Australians. To respond, Aborigines fein nods, muffle sounds, and use silence as "Marcel Marceau" strategies (Liberman, 1981). In order not to offend the questioner, the answer often approximates a "Might be!".

Similarly, black American children from inner-city areas may provide an apparently poor level of performance on forms of conservation tasks. They may furnish responses aimed to meet what they perceive to be the experimenter's needs and interpret "why" questions as a signal to change answers (Goodnow, 1984). This type of response may seem satisfactory to children who do not, or choose not to, understand the intent of the questioner. But it frustrates attempts at drawing out what children do know.

There are defences of interviewing children with questions that one would ask adolescents or adults. Leahy (1983), for example, has maintained that interviewing allows researchers to examine the structure and quality of children's justifications for their opinions. It may also reveal unexpected responses that would not be discovered using different methodologies. Yet as Leahy concedes, interviews are only a start and other techniques must be found to validate interview results.

But even though results from experiments which have used alternative methodologies have very often yielded contradictory results, interviewing continues to be used as a sole or primary source of knowledge about children. Many questions that require children to make judgements about their world inadvertently violate the rules of ordinary conversation that a speaker's messages should be sincere, informative, relevant, and non-redundant, and use linguistic forms which are clear and unambiguous in meaning. If listeners are inexperienced in the world of adult conversation, they may respond, for example, as if the speaker really meant that the properties of the objects to be compared, such as colour, are relevant to the correct answer. We cannot assume that children share the experimenter's definition of the attributes relevant to the task.

In sorting persons or objects into groups, young children typically rely on their own experiences. For example, Chi (1985) has described a study of a 5-year-old girl who was asked to sort the names of her classmates into groups. The groupings turned out to correspond to the seating order in the classroom. The girl was asked in a second study to sort and then to recall the names in alphabetical order with a list of the alphabet as a pointer. So long as the names were those of her classmates, she could easily retrieve a cluster of names beginning with the same letter. When asked to sort and recall names that did not represent classmates, but were nonetheless familiar, her recall was poor.

Children may need to connect their representation of their environment to the use of a new strategy. If knowledge is represented in a specific, familiar domain, even young children may be able to use concepts to sort things into organised taxonomies. Chi has reported the case of a 4-year-old who was an expert in his knowledge of dinosaurs. In his field, he was able to produce on request the names of 46 dinosaurs. A set of 40 was then chosen for further testing. Using the frequency of inclusion in the boy's nine dinosaur texts and his mother's judgement of his knowledge, the dinosaurs were divided into better known and lesser known groups. The boy could easily sort the 20 better known dinosaurs by food habits (meat-eaters and plant-eaters) and could categorise the dinosaurs further according to type of locomotion (e.g., two-legged, four-legged, or flying). These dimensions were more salient for the better known than for the lesser known groups, and guided the quick and exhaustive sorting behaviour of the expert boy.

Chi's findings once more clash with the position that young children are at a stage in which they suffer from a basic conceptual limitation. If a task is set in a relevant, co-operative, and informative atmosphere that abides by conversational rules, they will be more likely to demonstrate what they know.

Where the results of prolonged or unconventional questioning in interviews reveal a failure to understand, we often are left with the possibility that children are interpreting questions in ways different than those intended by the experimenter. Indeed, as Hughes and Grieve (1983) have shown, young children will seek to answer even the most bizarre questions. They will strain to make sense out of questions such as "Is milk bigger than water?" and "Is red heavier than yellow?" by importing a context of relevance into their replies: for example, "Yes, because there is more milk than water when you pour them into bottles" and "Yes, because red is darker than yellow". Similarly, adults can seek to answer questions that imply answers which are contrary to elementary logic. For example, Winer, Hemphill, and Craig (1988) had third graders, sixth graders, and college students to respond to misleading questions such as "When do you weigh the most, when you are walking or running?" Regardless of age, the majority selected one of the two incorrect choices rather than the logically correct response of rejecting the question and indicating that the weight remains the same.

Good experimental designs will avoid the possibility that children will use strategies of silence or gratuitous compliance. To reduce the difficulties inherent in interview studies and assist children to demonstrate the depth of their understanding, attractive, experimental contexts are often required in which they can produce and evaluate the rightness, truthfulness, and sincerity of responses in conversations.

ARE WE TAPPING INTO A FRACTION OF UNDERSTANDING?

Many young children can represent the invariant properties of number and length in conservation experiments and have insight into causal relations and the mental states of others. To what extent do they understand abstract concepts? The short answer to this question which was raised at the start of this essay is that children have a good deal more knowledge than they were credited with by Piaget. If so, in what sense are they fundamentally different from adult thinkers?

In an ambitious attempt to address the issue, Carey (1985a; 1985b) has argued that the major differences are in "domain-specific" knowledge. Children are novices and adults are experts in specific knowledge domains. Compared to adults, they simply know less about the world of number, peers, and so on. Consequently, children and adults hold different theories of the world. Once children identify, practice, and know when to use skills that permit problems to be solved, their theories become more adult-like.

Part of this process is "metaconceptual" or "metacognitive. Young children may not know when they should apply the knowledge that they already have or can have. They may not identify a need to acquire and use symbols to represent numbers, letters, and names. Another part is "metalinguistic". For example, children can understand messages guided by conversational rules better than messages that involve implicatures which depart from convention. It is difficult to see how children can accomplish metaconceptual tasks without first overcoming the metalinguistic problem of sharing the purpose and meaning of the experimenter.

To define competence in children's problem solving, Gelman, Meck, and Merkin (1986) have made a three-fold distinction. First, there is a "conceptual-competence" that characterises knowledge in specific domains such as counting. Second, there is a 'utilisation-competence" that involves the ability to determine the relevant features of the task and correctly interpret instructions. For example, on a counting task the child must appreciate that some displays have a clear beginning at the top or bottom where counters are arranged in rows while other displays in which counters are arranged in circles have no clear beginning. To avoid double-counting, the child must take note of this feature. Third, we have a "planning" or "procedural competence". This is the ability to select goals and strategies—for example, to co-ordinate the use of words for counting to tag each object to be counted only once with the goal of finding the correct cardinal number.

Knowing the goal to be achieved and knowing how to achieve it is different from knowing the correct solution. As Karmiloff-Smith (1986) points out, we can usefully examine knowledge in terms of that which is consciously accessible (sometimes called explicit or declarative knowledge, or roughly in Gelman's terms, conceptual knowledge) and that which can be implicitly represented in behaviour (sometimes called procedural knowledge). For example, in communication tasks, young children can implicitly identify linguistic forms such as sentences by responding correctly when they are asked to repeat the last sentence that they heard in a story. However, if asked directly and explicitly to say whether linguistic forms such as the articles "a" and "the" are words, they may not be able to reply explicitly. Similarly, children may have a substantial implicit knowledge of the AR distinction before possessing a conscious access to a dual representational code that is necessary to respond to direct AR questions. They may also have an implicit knowledge of fractions such as ½ and ¼ without consciously accessing symbols for fractions. Although they may not be able to state that 6 minus 4 equals 2, they will be likely to state the answer to a problem such as "There are 6 boys and 4 biscuits. How many boys will not have a biscuit?" Thus if an experimenter has the goal of examining the early capacity for representation through direct questioning about a remote or not clearly relevant matter, some children—even in non-redundant, single-task conditions—are liable to misinterpret the task requirements. Without knowing what to do, they are unlikely to demonstrate what they know. Since they may not consciously access their knowledge, they may represent appearance when asked to report reality or incorrectly represent whole numbers where fractions are required.

By contrast, children may demonstrate a procedural or implicit knowledge if the experimenter examines their understanding as a means to obtain a clear-cut goal such as the detection of pretence in familiar situations or the procurement of food and the avoidance of illness. Even many 2-year-olds, for example, may implicitly demonstrate knowledge of the distinction between appearance and reality by labelling as inedible food that appears safe but is contaminated in reality. Certainly, we would feel more secure in these circumstances if they could display a convincing explicit knowledge by spontaneously telling us that "Even if a drink looks OK it may have had a bug in it. So the drink may be contaminated." But to recognise that their knowledge in a domain may be mainly of the implicit sort is very different from embracing the conclusion that they have little or no understanding at all.

Yet experimenters can often seek explicit, declarative knowledge from children using methods which require still further explicit knowledge. In communication with adults, young children may initially operate under a "mental model" that does not represent departures from conversational rules. As Johnson-Laird (1983) has proposed, in making inferences listeners typically imagine a state of affairs based on the meaning of the premises. They then formulate an informative conclusion that corresponds to this state, and search for alternative models to test the validity of the conclusion. For young children, their experience in communication with adults often takes the form of the simple model: An A (adult) wants B (information) which can be found by asking C (child). The inference is simply that in questioning C (and C having co-operatively conveyed B to A), A has obtained the goal of knowing B.

But, for example, what if this mental model is disturbed by prolonged questioning on very similar tasks that sets aside the quantity rule that a speaker should speak no more than is required to communicate effectively? Children may not construct an alternative model based on the correct state of affairs: A wants to be sure that C knows about B and for this reason A uses redundant and prolonged techniques of questioning. Instead, they may operate on the basis of premises such as A believes that B can be found from C if C would change his or her mind, or that A was looking for a different B in the first place. Therefore, even if some children have an explicit or declarative understanding of a problem such as the knowledge that milk in a blue glass is white in reality and blue in appearance, it may not be conveyed in response to techniques that require the construction of an alternative model of the task and the experimenter's intentions.

According to Johnson-Laird (1983, pp. 126–145), we can distinguish between implicit and explicit inferential ability in interpreting discourse. Implicit inferences are based on a single or default mental model that processes information rapidly. Explicit inferences are required when the default model does not work and alternative models must be sought. Although young children are inexperienced in meeting this requirement, very often the strong claim is made that they are conceptually limited, that they have little or no understanding of features of the physical and social world, and that instruction in academic skills should be postponed until they attain a requisite stage of development. The use of unconventional or unfamiliar language that requires the explicit construction of alternative mental models may not only conceal an implicit knowledge of a problem but an explicit one as well.

The consequences of children's inexperience in constructing models of the experimenter's intent are serious, and mislead adults to tap into a fraction of their understanding. As I noted in Chapter Two, there are at least five possible explanations for their lack of success on many of the tasks that have been commonly used to characterise their inadequacies under prolonged, repeated, or other forms of questioning that set aside conversational rules where an answer may be perceived to be obvious or unobtainable.

1. "Switching Under Uncertainty".   Children who are uncertain of the answer in the first place may be induced to change their responses. For example, young children very often are inclined to conserve. But as in many matters, they can be less certain of the answer than older more experienced individuals. Under repeated questioning that is liable to stray from the quantity rule, they can be more easily led to comply with the suggestion that their first response may have been in error.

2. Insincerity.   Children may be certain of the answer. However, thay may respond incorrectly in an effort to end a conversation with a well-meaning experimenter who apparently does not accept their answers and to return to activities that are more attractive. For example, on conservation or AR tasks, children may be unwilling to repeat a correct response for an experimenter who has heard it before. If alternative activities are present, they may respond incorrectly just so that they can return to these.

3. The Overattractive Task Hypothesis.   Children again may be certain of the answer. However, contrary to the quantity and relevance rules, they may perceive the questions to be silly or to have obvious answers which require "cute" responses instead of correct ones. As in the case of adults' constant interest in gender-related matters, their answers to well-meaning questions about their gender concepts probably provide the ideal example. If alternative activities are unavailable, they may respond to attract the attention of adult questioners and to prolong the experiment.

4. Trust in the Experimenter.   Young children in the presence of adults are inclined not to be very bold. They are encouraged to defer to the directions and judgements of adults, particularly, for example, in health-related matters. Therefore, although at least some are knowledgeable about the invisible basis of contamination, they are not likely to question the motives of a grown-up who wants to test their knowledge about contaminants and have no grounds to assume that, contrary to the quality rule, they would be offered unsafe substances to eat or drink.

5. The Word-Use Hypothesis.   Children may not share adults' use of words or certain linguistic forms that are liable to infringe the manner rule to avoid ambiguity and obscurity. For example, they may interpret the word "same" to mean the "exact same" in size or dimension, or "number" to mean only whole numbers rather than fractions in referring to parts of circles, or "altogether" in word arithmetic problems to indicate "each".

Questionable questioning techniques may be employed whenever due regard is not given (1) to the implicit nature of much of children's early knowledge and (2) to their implicit reliance on a default model of communication compatible with Grice's Co-operative Principle and the rules or maxims for conversation (Quantity, Quality, Relevance, and Manner) which prescribe that a speaker should be sincere, informative, unambiguous, and say no more or no less than is required to elicit an answer.

Children's explicit inferential ability in interpreting discourse and the explicit knowledge of a subject matter warrants attention in itself and cannot be reduced to stages of memory development. In order to understand the meaning and purpose of the language used by an experimenter and to represent simultaneously different characteristics of a problem, children may remember to consider alternative mental models. Yet they may not realise which kind of model to construct and select.

For example, in two experiments on children's logical reasoning (Johnson-Laird, Oakhill, & Bull, 1986), 9- to 12-year-olds were given problems for which no alternative mental models could refute the validity of a conclusion and problems for which alternative mental models exist. For example, premises that require only one mental model to be constructed are "All the artists are beekeepers. All the beekeepers are chemists." No model exists to refute the conclusion: "All the artists are chemists." Children are significantly better at solving this sort of problem compared to one with premises such as: "Some of the artists are beekeepers. Some of the beekeepers are chemists." Although one model suggests the conclusion, "Some of the artists are chemists", explicit consideration needs to be given to an alternative that exists to refute it: "None of the artists are chemists." As predicted, the children's success at drawing valid conclusions from the premises was dependent on the number of mental models to be considered. However, the prediction that performance would be related to a measure of memory load (involving the transformation of sets of two and three letters to a designated later place in the alphabet) was not supported.

One may level the criticism that this sort of experiment is "ecologically invalid" because it uses premises that do not reflect everyday experiences and reasoning strategies. If this is so, how would the use of logic have come about in the first place? Moreover, as Johnson-Laird and his colleagues note, it is ironic to use a logical form of argument to criticise research on the use of logic. Their results highlight first, how mental models can guide effective problem solving and, second, that more than memory is involved in the use of models.

In fact, even very young children can be instructed to use models if the goal of the problem is made explicit and the context is made attractive. To examine the ability to transfer solutions across problems, Brown, Kane, and Echols (1986) read 3- to 5-year-olds a prototype problem about a Genie:

> A magic Genie lived for many years in a field behind a wall. His home was a very pretty bottle where he lived happily and collected a fine set of jewels. But one day an envious witch put a spell on the Genie. He was stuck to the spot, he couldn't move his feet, all his magic powers were gone. If he could move his home to the other side of the wall, he would be out of reach of the spell and his magic would come back. He had found an even prettier larger bottle on the other side, but he has a problem. How can he get his jewels across the high wall into the new bottle without breaking them and without moving his feet. The Genie has all these treasures to help him (glue, string, tape, etc.). Can you think of any way the Genie can get his jewels into the new bottle?

Children in a "recall" condition were asked to tell all they could remember about the story. Children in an "explicit goal structure" condition were given prompts to emphasise the abstract structure common to the Genie and subsequent transfer tasks: "Who has a problem? What did the Genie want to do? What is stopping the Genie? How did the Genie get his jewels across?" Compared to the recall group, those who were required to attend to the goal transferred their understanding across problems. In addition to their memory for story details, the knowledge of a common model contributed to their ability to transfer solutions.

Once again an explanation that rests upon the notion of a conceptual limitation in children's development does not fit their performance in experiments. To realise the skills that need to be employed in problem solving, children at times require prompting. If the goal is explicit and attractive, they will be more likely to access their knowledge as a means to achieve an end. If the goal is explicit, attractive, and familiar, they may do so even without prompting. If the means is incidental to achieving some relevant purpose, they will be more likely to know what is to be done and to know when and how to use their knowledge.

THE CHILD IN SOCIETY

Whichever way one looks at it, children are active producers of their environment. This was recognised by Piaget and is a significant advance over the behaviourist account, current in the first part of this century, that development is mainly the result of conditioning and reinforcement. Furthermore, Piaget has made an invaluable contribution in demonstrating the usefulness of experiments with children.

However, Piaget interpreted his results to support the existence of a basic conceptual limitation in early child development. Age differences in conservation answers, for example, were due to differences in the schema or functional architecture required to represent part-whole relations or to use concepts such as invariance. In adapting to the environment, he claimed that children later come to share the same logic or capacity for representation as adults. Despite many neo-Piagetians working in this tradition and the theoretical leaps taken by investigators of social development and education, recent experiments have challenged his analysis of children's knowledge. If we would have to deliver a verdict at this point in time, it would be that Piaget's developmental psychology frequently consists of a series of false negative results: his research methods have generated studies that have too often underestimated children's knowledge.

A systematic re-examination of the evidence requires adults to re-organise theories of development and models of knowledge. When children are studied in relation to their appreciation of conversational rules, we soon discover an early understanding of abstract concepts such as number, causality, and the identity of persons and objects that is in line with the talent which infants display in representing their environment. No longer can we ascribe to the simple (and perhaps for that reason, enticing) view that the emergence of abstract concepts is necessarily tied to some late-arriving stage where children at last emerge from their limitations.

In this sense, children do not stand apart from adult society. In granting that even preschoolers have an understanding of the physical and mental world, albeit one based on a restricted set of experiences, we find that an intensive involvement in early childhood is not misplaced. Preschoolers are not limited to superficial physical characteristics and can have friendships and peer relations based on a mutual knowledge of mental states.

The studies of Asian children that were mentioned in Chapter Six point to the effectiveness of parental involvement in promoting academic skills. Expectations for children vary cross-culturally. In contrast to the Asian situation, the conception of childhood in the West may reflect a complacency that—and I am conscious of a deliberate effort to be provocative here—is "infected" by a parental belief in stages or levels. Yet children's perceptions of parents, parenthood, and society may influence how and when they use their abilities (Siegal, 1985). Parental involvement and children's association with literate and numerate peers contributes to their academic achievement and concern for others. Of course a child's path in society is not determined as a preschooler or even in primary school. But a parental orientation that pays little attention to the active nature of the preschooler's reading and number skills can scarcely be expected to change radically as the child matures.

The challenge here is real and pressing. While we may legislate to prevent child abuse and to ensure that children attend school (though not necessarily to learn), it is more difficult to legislate that parents must give their children practice in identifying sounds and letters and in solving number problems—let alone to be sensitive to conversational rules that facilitate communication. Taxpayers may resist the suggestion that a desk be provided to students, even if they are children from poor families. The autonomy of parents to rear children in the way they see fit is a doctrine that is usually respected in Western society (see Eekelaar, 1984, for a discussion). We can only use techniques of persuasion in publicising the importance of the family context of development.

All the same, most parents are not familiar with issues in child development and research. Many do not consider whether children have the capacity to understand concepts. Nor do they strive for an ideal or detailed conception of the conditions under which children learn. Instead, their dealings with children are often influenced by a personal acquaintance with parent–child relationships. Accordingly, the quality of parental involvement may have its origin in early experiences, possibly in mothers' and fathers' childhood relationships with their own parents (Main, Kaplan, & Cassidy, 1985; Ricks, 1985; Slade, 1987).

Parenting is "habit-forming". A parental involvement that fosters academic skills in early childhood is more likely to be followed by high expectations and demands for the older child than in cases where parents have been comparatively non-involved. The involved parent of a preschooler who, for example, uses word and number games to help the child with reading and arithmetic, will more likely become the involved parent of a primary schooler. Moreover, parenting characteristics may be transmitted across generations so that parents' treatment of their children influences the upbringing of the next generation. In this respect, early experience may indirectly affect later human development.

In what way does a climate of parental involvement require a recognition of differences between parent–child communication and communication between adults? Hockett (1963), a linguist has listed design features for language and communication that are common to human speech in both adults and young children. Linguistic messages may refer to things and events that are distant in time and space (the design feature of "displacement"). New messages are coined freely and easily (the feature of "openness"). In addition, communication involves the ability to understand what has been termed "prevarication," the notion that linguistic messages can be false and meaningless. In many subject matters, children's knowledge may be more fragile than deep. But according to evidence from experiments, at least by the age of 4 years if not earlier, children have a concept of mental representation together with a capacity to understand false beliefs and to express the past and future. Therefore, they have an ability to use language to formulate and communicate hypotheses. Their conversation is guided by rules which are embedded in their spontaneous language development.

However, since children know less about adults' use of the rules of conversation and less about language generally, they may be more easily misled and their capacity for understanding left unrecognised. They are less likely to share an adult's intentions and goals for communication and the "implicatures" in adult conversation. At least to this extent, parent–child communication differs from communication between adults, and recognition ought to be accorded to a particular child's possible inexperience with the use of language, symbols, and departures from the conventional rules of conversation rather than to some unaccountable conceptual limitation. In this sense, conversational rules and children's interpretation of the meaning and purpose of language are a building block for theories of child development, and for a developmental cognitive science that embraces linguistics, philosophy, psychology, and related disciplines.

Children's knowledge of the intent underlying departures from conventional methods of questioning—the conversational implicatures used by adults—may develop later. With intensive daily experience at home and school, they come to understand when, for example, the quantity rule can be violated deliberately with tact and politeness as a form of implicature for the purpose of obtaining clarification. Indeed, languages in some cultures such as Australian Aboriginal groups are based on this notion, with repeated questioning enshrined in communication patterns (Liberman, 1981; Siegal,1988b).

Of course there is more to development that the ability to share purposes and meanings in experimental settings. Even if children understand the conversational context of the task and are not misled by unfamiliar language, and would know how and when to apply the solution if they had it, they may still lack the conceptual competence—the logico-mathematical knowledge and principles—to succeed fully. Only a skeletal understanding may be present and experimenters must be wary to steer between two errors: to avoid false negatives in claiming that children do not know when they actually do, and to avoid false positives in claiming that they do know when they actually do not. To ensure that a conceptual limitation in development is deep rather than superficial, it is necessary to rule out explanations for negative results. Ways are required to test the rival hypotheses that children's lack of performance is due to ambiguity in questioning, certain perceptions of the experimenter and task, and unfamiliar language that does not map on to children's theories of the mental and physical world. These methods may include having children offer causal attributions for peers' responses, placing tasks in relevant (e.g., food-related) contexts, and simplifying linguistic forms by pairing numbers with pictures. An approach that focuses on the language of the experiment and the presence of an early implicit knowledge harbours the possibility of discovering more capacity in children's understanding than has often been envisioned.

In line with Helmholtz's notion of unconscious, perceptual inferences, many experiments have now revealed a subtle understanding that is implicit in infants and young children. Similarly, Darwin's emphasis on the diversity of species in adapting to their environment is a forerunner to modern studies on biological constraints that promote learning. In their accolade to Darwin, Rozin and Schull (1988) enumerate four broad categories of "fitness-promoting" activities in biological organisms: sheltering, predator avoidance, nutrient procurement, and parenting. Experiments have supported the notion that constraints towards the learning of these behaviours are present in young children. The early understanding of objects in space, time, and mental states forms a basis for sheltering and predator avoidance. The very early knowledge of the distinction between appearance and reality in the context of food and contamination sensitivity surely contributes to the procurement of nutrients. Then there is continuity between generations and the ability of young children to discern and evaluate authority in sustaining patterns of parenting behaviour.

Nevertheless, psychologists and educators are far short of charting the full extent of children's capacity for understanding. To date, it is true, in searching for original states and for mechanisms of change, an impressive depth of understanding has been uncovered. Through experiments, it is known that child development is better characterised by development towards a conscious accessibility of implicit knowledge rather than a simple lack of conceptual knowledge or coherence at different stages. However, important gaps remain—ones that are larger than the outline of development that has been provided up to now. It remains easier to state what should not be included in models of knowledge in young children than what should be. It is easier to state descriptions than to offer explanations of developmental changes.

Studies of children's number and reading, their understanding of health, illness, and safety, their ability to represent viewpoints and causal relations, and their conceptions of authority and friendship are areas for research on development. Only a start has been made and much remains to be done. The task ahead is to negotiate an account of development guided by breadth, depth, and vision. At the same time, it is to promote communication in knowing children.

References

Ackerman, B.P. (1981). When is a question not answered? The understanding of young children of utterances violating or conforming to the rules of conversational sequencing. *Journal of Experimental Child Psychology*, *31*, 487–507.

Allport, G.W. & Postman L. (1947). *The psychology of rumor*. New York: Henry Holt.

Antell, S.E. & Keating, D.P. (1983). Perception of numerical invariance in neonates. *Child Development*, *54*, 695–701.

Asch, S.E. (1958). Effects of group pressure upon the modification and distortion of judgments. In E.E. Maccoby, T.M. Newcomb, & E.L. Hartley (Eds.), *Readings in social psychology*, Third edition. New York: Henry Holt.

Asher, S.R. & Dodge, K.A. (1986). Identifying children who are rejected by their peers. *Developmental Psychology*, *22*, 444–449.

Asher, S.R. & Wheeler, V.A. (1985). Children's loneliness: A comparison of rejected and neglected peer status. *Journal of Consulting and Clinical Psychology*, *53*, 500–505.

Baillargeon, R. & Graber, M. (1988). Evidence of location memory in 8-month-old infants in a nonsearch AB task. *Developmental Psychology*, *24*, 502–511.

Baillargeon, R., Spelke, E.S., & Wasserman, S. (1985). Object permanence in five-month-old infants. *Cognition*, *20*, 191–208.

Baumrind, D. (1983). Rejoinder to Lewis's reinterpretation of parental control effects: Are authoritative parents really harmonious? *Psychological Bulletin*, *94*, 132–142.

Berger, M. (1985). *Germs make me sick*. New York: Harper and Row.

Bertoncini, J., Bijeljac-Babic, R., Jusczyk, P.W., Kennedy, L.J., & Mehler, J. (1988). *Journal of Experimental Psychology: General*, *117*, 21–33.

Bibace, R. & Walsh, M.E. (1981). Children's conceptions of illness. In R. Bibace & M. Walsh (Eds.), *New directions for child development: Children's conceptions of health, illness, and bodily functions, No. 14*. San Francisco: Jossey-Bass.

Block, J.H. (1983). Differential premises arising from differential socialization of the sexes: Some conjectures. *Child Development*, *54*, 1335–1354.

Borges, J.L. (1964). *Labyrinths*. New York: New Directions.

Borke, H. (1975). Piaget's mountains revisited: Changes in the egocentric landscape. *Developmental Psychology, 11*, 240–243.

Braine, M.D.S. & Rumain, B. (1983). Logical reasoning. In P.H. Mussen (Ed.), *Handbook of child psychology, Vol. 3* (pp. 263–340; J.H. Flavell & E.M. Markman, Vol. Eds.). New York: Wiley.

Brandt, A.M. (1987). *No magic bullet*. New York: Oxford University Press.

Bremner, J.G. & Knowles, L.S. (1984). Piagetian stage IV search errors with an object that is directly accesible both visually and manually. *Perception, 13*, 307–314.

Bronstein, P. (1984). Differences in mothers' and fathers' behaviors toward children: A cross-cultural comparison. *Developmental Psychology, 20*, 995–1003.

Brown, A.L., Kane, M.J., & Echols, C.H. (1986). Young children's mental models determine analogical transfer across problems with a common goal structure. *Cognitive Development, 1*, 103–121.

Brown, P. & Levinson, S.C. (1987). *Politeness: Some universals in language usage*. Cambridge: Cambridge University Press.

Bryant, P.E. (1974). *Perception and understanding in young children*. London: Methuen.

Bryant, P.E. (1985). The distinction between knowing when to do a sum and knowing how to do it. *Educational Psychology, 5*, 207–215.

Bryant, P.E. & Bradley, L. (1983). *Children's reading problems*. Oxford: Blackwell.

Bryant, P.E., Jones, P., Claxton, V., & Perkins, G.M. (1972). Recognition of shapes across modalities by infants. *Nature, 240*, 303–304.

Bryant, P.E. & Kopytynska, H. (1976). Spontaneous measurement by young children. *Nature, 260*, 773.

Bullock, M. (1985). Animism in childhood thinking: A new look at an old question. *Developmental Psychology, 21*, 217–225.

Burbach, D.J. & Peterson, L. (1986). Children's concepts of physical illness: A review and critique of the cognitive–developmental literature. *Health Psychology, 5*, 307–325.

Butterworth, G. & Hopkins, B. (1988). Hand–mouth coordination in the new-born baby. *British Journal of Developmental Psychology, 6*, 303–314.

Carey, S. (1985a). Are children fundamentally different kinds of thinkers and learners than adults? In S.F. Chipman, J.W. Segal, & J.R. Glaser (Eds.), *Thinking and learning skills, Vol. 2*. Hillsdale, N.J.: Lawrence Erlbaum Associates Inc.

Carey, S. (1985b). *Conceptual change in childhood*. Cambridge, Mass.: Bradford Books/ MIT Press.

Case, R. (1985). *Intellectual development: Birth to adulthood*. Orlando, Fla.: Academic Press.

Ceci, S.J., Ross, D.F., & Toglia, M.P. (1987). Suggestibility of children's memory: Psycho-legal implications. *Journal of Experimental Psychology: General, 116*, 38–49.

Chi, M.T.H. (1985). Interactive roles of knowledge and strategies in the development of organized sorting and recall. In S.F. Chipman, J.W. Segal, & R. Glaser (Eds), *Thinking and learning skills, Vol. 2*. Hillsdale, N.J.: Lawrence Erlbaum Associates Inc.

Cohen, L.J. (1971). Some remarks on Grice's views about the logical particles of natural language. In Y. Bar-Hillel (Ed.), *Pragmatics of natural language*. Dordrecht, Holland: D. Reidel.

Coie, J.D., Dodge, K.A., & Coppotelli, H. (1982). Dimensions and types of social status: A cross-age perspective. *Developmental Psychology, 18*, 557–570.

Coie, J.D. & Krehbiel, G. (1984). Effects of academic tutoring on the social status of low-achieving, socially rejected children. *Child Development, 55*, 1465–1478.

Coie, J.D. & Kupersmidt, J.B. (1983). A behavioral analysis of emerging social status in boys' groups. *Child Development, 54*, 1400–1416.

Content, A., Kolinsky, R., Morais, J., & Bertelson, P. (1986). Phonetic segmentation in prereaders: Effect of corrective information. *Journal of Experimental Child Psychology, 42*, 49–72.

Cummins, D.D., Kintsch, W., Reusser, K., & Weimer, R. (1988). The role of understanding in solving word arithmetic problems. *Cognitive Psychology*, *20*, 405–438.

Dahl, R. (1959). *Kiss, Kiss*. New York: Knopf.

Dalenberg, C.J., Bierman, K.L., & Furman, W. (1984). A reexamination of developmental changes in causal attributions. *Developmental Psychology*, *20*, 575–583.

Darwin, C.R. (1859). *On the origins of species by means of natural selection, or the preservation of favoured races in the struggle for life*. London: John Murray.

DeCasper, A.J. & Fifer, W.P. (1980). Of human bonding: Newborns prefer their mother's voice. *Science*, *208*, 1174–1176.

DeLoache, J.S. (1987). Rapid change in the symbolic functioning of very young children. *Science*, *238*, 1556–1557.

Denham, S.A. (1986). Social cognition, prosocial behavior, and emotion in preschoolers: Contextual validation. *Child Development*, *57*, 194–201.

DeVries, R. (1969). Constancy of generic identity in the years three to six. *Monographs of the Society for Research in Child Development*, *34*, Serial No. 127.

Diamond, A. (1985). The development of the ability to use recall to guide action, as indicated by infants' performance on AB. *Child Development*, *56*, 868–883.

Dix, T. & Grusec, J.E. (1983). Parental influence techniques: An attributional analysis. *Child Development*, *54*, 645–652.

Dodge, K.A. (1983). Behavioral antecedents of peer social status. *Child Development*, *54*, 1386–1399.

Dodge, K.A. (1985). A social information processing model of social competence in children. In M. Perlmutter (Ed.), *Minnesota Symposium on Child Psychology, Vol. 18*. Hillsdale, N.J.: Lawrence Erlbaum Associates Inc.

Dodge, K.A., Coie, J.D., & Brakke, N.P. (1982). Behavior patterns of socially rejected and neglected preadolescents: The roles of social approach and aggression. *Journal of Abnormal Child Psychology*, *10*, 389–410.

Dodge, K.A. & Somberg, D.R. (1987). Hostile attributional biases among aggressive boys are exacerbated under conditions of threat to the self. *Child Development*, *58*, 213–224.

Dolgin, K. & Behrend, D. (1984). Children's knowledge about animates and inanimates. *Child Development*, *55*, 1646–1650.

Donaldson, M. (1978). *Children's minds*. Glasgow: Fontana.

Donaldson, M. & Balfour, G. (1968). Less is more: A study of language comprehension in children. *British Journal of Psychology*, *59*, 461–471.

Dunn, J., Bretherton, I., & Munn, P. (1987). Conversations about feeling states between mothers and their young children. *Developmental Psychology*, *23*, 132–139.

Eades, D. (1982). You gotta know how to talk . . . Information seeking in South-East Queensland Aboriginal Society. *Australian Journal of Linguistics*, *2*, 61–82.

Eekelaar, J. (1984). *Family law and social policy*, second edition. London: Weidenfeld and Nicolson.

Eimas, P.D. & Miller, J.L. (1980). Contextual effects in infant speech perception. *Science*, *209*, 1140–1141.

Eiser, C. (1985). *The psychology of childhood illness*. New York: Springer-Verlag.

Enright, R.D., Enright, W.F., & Lapsley, D.K. (1981). Distributive justice and social class: A replication. *Developmental Psychology*, *17*, 826–832.

Enright, R.D. & Sutterfield, S.J. (1980). An ecological validation of social cognitive development. *Child Development*, *51*, 156–161.

Fallon, A.E., Rozin, P., & Pliner, P. (1984). The child's conception of food rejections with special reference to disgust and contamination sensitivity. *Child Development*, *55*, 566–575.

Field, T.M., Woodson, R., Greenberg, R., & Cohen, D. (1982). Discrimination and imitation of facial expressions by neonates. *Science*, *218*, 179–181.

Flavell, J.H., Everett, B.A., Croft, K., & Flavell, E.R. (1981). Young children's knowledge about visual perception: Further evidence for the Level 1–Level 2 distinction. *Developmental Psychology, 17,* 99–103.

Flavell, J.H., Flavell, E.R., & Green, F.L. (1983). Development of the appearance–reality distinction. *Cognitive Psychology, 15,* 95–120.

Flavell, J.H., Flavell, E.R., & Green, F.L. (1989). Young children's ability to differentiate appearance–reality and Level 2 perspectives in the tactile modality. *Child Development, 60,* 201–213.

Flavell, J.H., Green, F.L., & Flavell, E.R. (1986). Development of the appearance–reality distinction. *Monographs of the Society for Research in Child Development, 51,* Serial No. 212.

Flavell, J.H., Green, F.L., Wahl, K.E., & Flavell, E.R. (1987). The effects of question clarification and memory aids on young children's performance on appearance–reality tasks. *Cognitive Development, 2,* 127–144.

Fluck, M. & Hewison, Y. (1979). The effect of televised presentation on number conservation in 5-year-olds. *British Journal of Psychology, 70,* 507–509.

Ford, M.E. (1979). The construct validity of egocentrism. *Psychological Bulletin, 86,* 1169–1188.

Ford, M.E. (1985). Two perspectives on the validation of developmental constructs: Psychometric and theoretical limitation in research on egocentrism. *Psychological Bulletin, 97,* 497–501.

Freeman, N.H., Lloyd, S., & Sinha, C.G. (1980). Infant search tasks reveal early concepts of containment and canonical use of objects. *Cognition, 8,* 243–262.

Freeman, N.H., Sinha, C.G., & Condliffe, S.G. (1981). Collaboration and confrontation with young children in language comprehension testing. In W.P. Robinson (Ed.), *Communication and development.* London: Academic Press.

Friedman, W.J. (1988). *Children's knowledge of the duration of familiar events.* Unpublished manuscript, Oberlin College.

Frege, G. (1884/1953). *Foundations of arithmetic.* Oxford: Basil Blackwell.

Frege, G. (1960). *Translations from the philosophical writings of Gottlob Frege.* Oxford: Basil Blackwell.

French, D.C. & Waas, G.A. (1985). Behavior problems of peer-neglected and peer-rejected elementary-age children: Parent and teacher perspectives. *Child Development, 56,* 246–252.

Furman, W. & Bierman, K.L. (1983). Developmental changes in young children's conceptions of friendship. *Child Development, 54,* 549–556.

Furman, W. & Masters, J.C. (1980). Peer interactions, sociometric status, and resistance to deviations in young children. *Developmental Psychology, 16,* 229–236.

Furth, H.G. & Wachs, H. (1974). *Thinking goes to school: Piaget's theory in practice.* New York: Oxford University Press.

Fuson, K. (1986a). Roles of representation and verbalization in the teaching of multi-digit addition and subtraction. *European Journal of the Psychology of Education, 1,* 35–56.

Fuson, K.C. (1986b). Teaching children to subtract by counting up. *Journal for Research in Mathematics Education, 17,* 172–189.

Gelman, R. (1982). Accessing one-to-one correspondence: Still another paper about conservation. *British Journal of Psychology, 73,* 209–220.

Gelman, R. & Gallistel, C.R. (1978). *The child's understanding of number.* Cambridge, Mass.: Harvard University Press.

Gelman, R. & Meck, E. (1983). Preschoolers' counting: Principles before skill. *Cognition, 13,* 343–359.

Gelman, R., Meck, E., & Merkin, S. (1986). Young children's numerical competence. *Cognitive Development, 1,* 1–29.

Gelman, R. & Shatz, M. (1977). Appropriate speech adjustments: The operation of conversational constraints on talk to two-year-olds. In M. Lewis & L.A. Rosenblum (Eds.), *Interaction, conversation, and the development of language*. New York: Wiley.

Gelman, S.A., Collman, P., & Maccoby, E.E. (1986). Inferring properties from categories versus inferring categories from properties: The case of gender. *Child Development, 57*, 396–404.

Gershman, E.S. & Hayes, D.S. (1983). Differential stability of reciprocal relationships among preschool children. *Merrill-Palmer Quarterly, 29*, 169–177.

Gibson, E.J. & Walker, A.S. (1984). Development of knowledge of visual-factual affordance of substance. *Child Development, 55*, 453–460.

Glick, J. (1978). Cognition and social cognition: An introduction. In J. Glick & K.A. Clarke-Stewart (Eds.), *The development of social understanding*. New York: Gardner Press.

Goodman, G.S., Golding, J.M., & Haith, M.M. (1984). Jurors' reactions to child witnesses. *Journal of Social Issues, 40*, 139–156.

Goodnow, J.J. (1984). On being judged "intelligent". *International Journal of Psychology, 19*, 391–406.

Goodnow, J.J. (1988). Parents' ideas, actions, and feelings: Methods and models from developmental and social psychology. *Child Development, 59*, 286–320.

Goswami, U. (1986). Children's use of analogy in learning to read: A developmental study. *Journal of Experimental Child Psychology, 42*, 73–83.

Grice, H.P. (1975). Logic and conversation. In P. Cole & J.L. Morgan (Eds.), *Syntax and semantics, Vol. 3: Speech acts*. New York: Academic Press.

Grolnick, W.S. & Ryan, R.M. (1986). *Parent styles associated with children's school-related adjustment and competence*. Unpublished paper, University of Rochester.

Halford, G.S. & Boyle, F.M. (1985). Do young children understand conservation of number? *Child Development, 56*, 165–173.

Harner, L. (1975). Yesterday and tomorrow: Development of early understanding of the terms. *Developmental Psychology, 11*, 864–865.

Harris, P.L., Donnelly, K., Gaz, G.R., & Pitt-Watson, R. (1986). Children's understanding of the distiction between real and apparent emotion. *Child Development, 57*, 895–909.

Hartup, W.W. (1983). Peer relations. In P.H. Mussen (Series Ed.) & E.M. Hetherington (Vol. Ed.), *Handbook of Child Psychology, Vol. IV*. New York: Wiley.

Hewison, J. & Tizard, J. (1980). Parental involvement and reaching attainment. *British Journal of Educational Psychology, 50*, 209–215.

Higgins, E.T. (1981). Role-taking and social judgment: Alternative developmental perspectives and processes. In J.H. Flavell & L. Ross (Eds.), *Social cognitive development: Frontiers and possible futures*. New York: Cambridge University Press.

Higgins, E.T., Feldman, N.S., & Ruble, D.N. (1980). Accuracy and differentiation in social prediction: A developmental perspective. *Journal of Personality, 48*, 520–540.

Hockett, C.F. (1963). The problem of universals in language. In J.H. Greenberg (Ed.), *Universals in language*. Cambridge, Mass.: MIT Press.

Hoffman, M.L. (1970). Moral development. In P. Mussen (Ed.), *Carmichael's manual of child psychology*, Vol. II, third edition. New York: Wiley.

Hudson, T. (1983). Correspondences and numerical differences between disjoint sets. *Child Development, 54*, 84–90.

Hughes, M. (1986). *Children and number*. Oxford: Blackwell.

Hughes, M. & Grieve, R. (1983). On asking children bizarre questions. In M. Donaldson, R. Grieve, & C. Pratt (Eds.), *Child development and education*. Oxford: Blackwell.

Huston, A.C. (1983). Sex-typing. In P.H. Mussen (Series Ed.) & E.M. Hetherington (Vol. Ed.), *Handbook of child psychology*, Vol. 4, fourth edition. New York: Wiley.

Hymel, S. (1983). Preschool children's peer relations: Issues in sociometric assessment. *Merrill-Palmer Quarterly, 29*, 237–260.

Inhelder, B. & Piaget, J. (1985). *Growth of logical thinking from childhood to adolescence.* New York: Basic Books.

James, W. (1960). *The principles of psychology.* New York: Dover (originally published 1890).

Johnson, C.N. & Wellman, H.M. (1982). Children's developing conceptions of the mind and the brain. *Child Development, 53*, 222–234.

Johnson, J.E. & McGillicuddy-Delisi, A. (1983). Family environment factors and children's knowledge of rules and conventions. *Child Development, 54*, 218–226.

Johnson, M.K. & Foley, M.A. (1984). Differentiating fact from fantasy: The reliability of children's memory. *Journal of Social Issues, 40*, 33–50.

Johnson, M.M. (1963). Sex role learning in the nuclear family. *Child Development, 34*, 315–333.

Johnson, M.M. (1975). Fathers, mothers, and sex typing. *Sociological Inquiry, 45*, 15–26.

Johnson-Laird, P.N. (1983). *Mental models.* Cambridge, Mass.: Harvard University Press.

Johnson-Laird, P.N., Oakhill, J., & Bull, D. (1986). Children's syllogistic reasoning. *Quarterly Journal of Experimental Psychology, 38A*, 35–58.

Karmiloff-Smith, A. (1986). From meta-processes to conscious access: Evidence from children's metalinguistic and repair data. *Cognition, 23*, 95–147.

Karniol, R. & Ross, M. (1976). The development of causal attributions in social perception. *Journal of Personality and Social Psychology, 34*, 455–464.

Keil, F.C. (1979). *Semantic and conceptual development: An ontological perspective.* Cambridge, Mass.: Harvard University Press.

Keil, F.C. (1983). On the emergence of semantic and conceptual distinctions. *Journal of Experimental Psychology: General, 112*, 357–385.

Kelley, H.H. (1973). The process of causal attribution. *American Psychologist, 28*, 107–128.

Kellman, P.J., Spelke, E.S., & Short, K.R. (1986). Infant perception of object unity from translatory motion in depth and vertical translation. *Child Development, 57*, 72–86.

Kister, M.C. & Patterson, C.J. (1980). Children's conceptions of the causes of illness: Understanding of contagion and use of immanent justice. *Child Development, 51*, 839–846.

Kleinman, A. (1986). Some uses and misuses of the social sciences in medicine. In D.W. Fiske & R.A. Shweder (Eds.), *Metatheory in social science.* Chicago: University of Chicago Press.

Kohlberg, L. (1966). A cognitive-developmental analysis of children's sex-role concepts and attitudes. In E.E. Maccoby (Ed.), *The development of sex differences.* Stanford, Calif.: Stanford University Press.

Kohlberg, L. & Ullian, D. (1974). Stages in the development of psychosexual concepts and attitudes. In R.C. Friedman, R.M. Richart, & R.L. Van de Wiele (Eds.), *Sex differences in behavior.* New York: Wiley.

Kuczaj, S.A. (1975). On the acquisition of a semantic system. *Journal of Verbal Learning and Verbal Behavior, 14*, 340–358.

Kuzmak, S.D. & Gelman, R. (1986). Young children's understanding of random phenomena. *Child Development, 57*, 559–566.

Ladd, G.W. (1983). Social networks of popular, average, and rejected children in school settings. *Merrill-Palmer Quarterly, 29*, 283–307

Ladd, G.W., Price, J.M., & Hart, C.H. (1988). Predicting preschoolers' peer status from their playground behaviors. *Child Development, 59*, 986–992.

Lampert, M. (1986). Knowing, doing, and teaching multiplication. *Cognition and Instruction, 3*, 305–342.

Langlois, J.H. & Downs, J.H. (1980). Mothers, fathers, and peers as socialization agents of sex-typed play behaviors in young children. *Child Development*, *51*, 1217–1247.

Leahy, R.L. (1983). Development of the conception of economic inequality, II: Explanations, justifications, and concepts of social mobility and change. *Developmental Psychology*, *19*, 111–125.

Leech, G. (1983). *Principles of pragmatics*. London: Longman.

Lepper, M.R. (1983). Social-control processes and the internalization of social values: An attributional perspective. In E.T. Higgins, D.N. Ruble, & W.W. Hartup (Eds.), *Social cognition and social development: A sociocultural perspective*. New York: Cambridge University Press.

Lepper, M.R. & Gilovich, M.R. (1981). The multiple functions of reward: A social-developmental perspective. In S.S. Brehm, S.M. Kassin, & F.X. Gibbons (Eds.), *Developmental social psychology*. New York: Oxford University Press.

Leslie, A.M. (1987). Pretense and representation: The origins of "theory of mind". *Psychological Review*, *94*, 412–426.

Leslie, A.M. & Keeble, S. (1987). Do six-month-old infants perceive causality? *Cognition*, *25*, 265–288.

Levin, I. (1982). The nature and development of time. In W.J. Friedman (Ed.), *The developmental psychology of time*. New York: Academic Press.

Lewis, C.C. (1981). The effects of parental firm control: A reinterpretation. *Psychological Bulletin*, *90*, 547–563.

Lewis, M. & Sullivan, M.W. (1985). Imitation in the first six months of life. *Merrill-Palmer Quarterly*, *31*, 315–333.

Liberman, K. (1981). Understanding Aborigines in Australian courts of law. *Human Organization*, *40*, 247–255.

Liben, L. (1978). Perspective-taking skills in young children: Seeing the world through rose-colored glasses. *Developmental Psychology*, *14*, 87–92.

Light, P.H., Buckingham, N., & Robins, A.H. (1979). The conservation task in an interactional setting. *British Journal of Educational Psychology*, *49*, 304–310.

Lynn, D.B. (1959). A note on sex differences in the development of masculine and feminine identification. *Psychological Review*, *66*, 126–135.

Lynn, D.B. (1962). Sex role and parental identification. *Child Development*, *33*, 555–564.

Maccoby, E.E. & Jacklin, C.N. (1974). *The psychology of sex differences*. Stanford, Calif.: Stanford University Press.

Macnamara, J. (1982). *Names for Things*. Cambridge, Mass.: Bradford Books/MIT.

Macnamara, J. (1986). *A border dispute: The place of logic in psychology*. Cambridge, Mass.: MIT Press.

Maddux, J.E., Roberts, M.C., Sledden, E.A., & Wright, L. (1986). Developmental issues in child health psychology. *American Psychologist*, *41*, 25–34.

Main, M., Kaplan, N., & Cassidy, J. (1985). Security in infancy, childhood, and adulthood: A move to the level of representation. In I. Bretherton & E. Waters (Eds.), Growing points of attachment theory and research. *Monographs of the Society for Research in Child Development*, *50*, Serial No. 209, 66–104.

Mandler, J.M. (1987). How to build a baby: On the development of an accessible representational system. *Cognitive Development*, *3*, 113–136.

Marcus, D.E. & Overton, W.F. (1978). The development of cognitive gender constancy and sex role preferences. *Child Development*, *49*, 434–444.

Martin, C.L. & Halverson, C.F. (1981). A schematic processing model of sex typing and stereotyping in children. *Child Development*, *52*, 1119–1134.

Martin, C.L. & Halverson, C.F. (1983). Gender constancy: A methodological and theoretical analysis. *Sex Roles*, *9*, 775–790.

Massey, C. & Gelman, R. (1988). Preschoolers' ability to decide whether a pictured unfamiliar object can move itself. *Developmental Psychology, 24*, 307–317.

Masten, A.S. (1986). Humor and competence in school-aged children. *Child Development, 57*, 461–473.

Matsumoto, Y. (1988). Re-examination of the universality of face: Politeness phenomena in Japanese. *Journal of Pragmatics, 12*, 403–426.

McGarrigle, J., Grieve, R., & Hughes, M. (1978). Interpreting inclusion: A contribution to the study of the child's cognitive and linguistic development. *Journal of Experimental Child Psychology, 25*, 528–550.

McGee, R., Williams, S., Share, D.L., Anderson, J., & Silva, P.A. (1986). The relationship between specific reading retardation, general reading backwardness and behavioural problems in a large sample of Dunedin boys: A longitudinal study from five to eleven years. *Journal of Child Psychology and Psychiatry, 27*, 597–610.

McGuire, K.D. & Weisz, J.R. (1982). Social cognition and behavior correlates preadolescent chumship. *Child Development, 53*, 1478–1484.

McKenzie, B. & Over, R. (1983). Young infants fail to imitate facial and manual gestures. *Infant Behavior and Development, 2*, 85–93.

Meltzoff, A. & Borton, R.W. (1979). Intermodal matching by human neonates. *Nature, 282*, 403–404.

Meltzoff, A. & Moore, M.K. (1977). Imitation of facial and manual gestures by human neonates. *Science, 218*, 179–181.

Mendleson, M.J. & Haith, M.M. (1976). The relation between audition and vision in the newborn. *Monographs of the Society for Research in Child Development, 41*, Serial No. 167.

Miller, S.A. (1986). Parents' beliefs about their children's cognitive abilities. *Developmental Psychology, 22*, 276–284.

Miller, S.A. (1988). Parents' beliefs about children's cognitive development. *Child Development, 59*, 259–285.

Murdock, G.P. (1980). *Theories of illness: A world survey*. Pittsburgh: University of Pittsburgh Press.

Neilson, I., Dockrell, J., & McKechnie, J. (1983). Does repetition of the question influence children's performance in conservation tasks? *British Journal of Developmental Psychology, 1*, 163–174.

Newcomb, A.F. & Bukowski, W.M. (1984). A longitudinal study of the utility of social preference and social impact sociometric classification schemes. *Child Development, 55*, 1434–1447.

Nisan, M. (1987). Moral norms and social conventions: A cross-cultural comparison. *Developmental Psychology, 23*, 719–725.

Nisan, M. (1988). A story of a pot, or a cross-cultural comparison of basic moral evaluations: A response to the critique by Turiel, Nucci, and Smetana (1988). *Developmental Psychology, 24*, 144–146.

Nucci, L. & Nucci, M.S. (1982). Children's social interactions in the context of moral and conventional transgressions. *Child Development, 53*, 403–412.

Nucci, L. & Turiel, E. (1978). Social interactions and the development of social concepts in preschool children. *Child Development, 49*, 400–407.

Passingham, R.E. (1982). *The human primate*. Oxford: W.H. Freeman.

Peery, J.C. (1979). Popular, amiable, isolated, rejected: A reconceptualization of sociometric status in preschool children. *Child Development, 50*, 1231–1234.

Perner, J., Leekam, S.R. & Wimmer, H. (1986). *The insincerity of conservation questions: Children's growing insensitivity to experimenter's intentions*. Unpublished manuscript. University of Sussex.

Perner, J., Leekam, S.R., & Wimmer, H. (1987). Three year olds' difficulty with false belief: The case for a conceptual deficit. *British Journal of Developmental Psychology*, *5*, 125–137.

Perner, J. & Ogden, J.E. (1988). Hunger for knowledge: Children's problem with representation in imputing mental states. *Cognition*, *29*, 47–61.

Petitto, L.A. (1986). "Language" in the prelinguistic child. In F. Kessel (Ed.), *The development of language and language researchers*. Hillsdale, N.J.: Lawrence Erlbaum Associates Inc.

Piaget, J. (1928). *Judgment and reasoning in the child*. London: Routledge & Kegan Paul.

Piaget, J. (1929). *The child's conception of the world*. London: Routledge & Kegan Paul.

Piaget, J. (1930). *The child's conception of physical causality*. London: Routledge & Kegan Paul.

Piaget, J. (1932). *The moral judgment of the child*. London: Routledge & Kegan Paul.

Piaget, J. (1952). *The child's conception of number*. London: Routledge & Kegan Paul.

Piaget, J. (1954). *The construction of reality in the child*. New York: Basic Books.

Piaget, J. (1969). *The child's conception of time*. London: Routledge & Kegan Paul.

Piaget, J. (1970). Piaget's theory. In P.H. Mussen (Ed.), *Carmichael's manual of child psychology, Vol. 1*. New York: Wiley.

Piaget, J. (1972). Piaget sees science dooming psychoanalysis. *New York Times*, October 19th.

Piaget, J. & Inhelder, B. (1956). *The child's conception of space*. New York: Norton.

Piaget, J., Inhelder, B., & Szeminska, A. (1964). *The child's conception of geometry*. New York: Harper Torchbook.

Presson, C.C. & Ihrig, L.H. (1982). Using mother as a spatial landmark: Evidence against egocentric coding in infancy. *Developmental Psychology*, *18*, 699–703.

Pylyshyn, Z.W. (1984). *Computation and cognition*. Cambridge, Mass.: MIT Press.

Resnick, L.B. & Ford, W.W. (1981). *The psychology of mathematics for instruction*. Hillsdale, N.J.: Lawrence Erlbaum Associates Inc.

Ricks, M.H. (1985). The social transmission of parental behavior: Attachment across generations. In I. Bretherton & E. Waters (Eds.), Growing points of attachment theory and research. *Monographs of the Society for Research in Child Development*, *50*, Serial No. 209, 211–227.

Rogoff, B. & Wertsch, J.V. (Eds.) (1984). *Children's learning in the "Zone of proximal development"*. New Directions for Child Development, No. 23. San Francisco: Jossey-Bass.

Rose, S.A. & Blank, M, (1974). The potency of context in childrens cognition: An illustration through conservation. *Child Development*, *45*, 499–502.

Rosenberg, C.E. (1962). *The cholera years: The United States in 1832 and 1866*. Chicago: University of Chicago Press.

Rothbaum, F., Weisz, J.R., & Snyder, S.S. (1982). Changing the world and changing the self: A two-process model of perceived control. *Journal of Personality and Social Psychology*, *42*, 5–37.

Rozin, P. (1976). The evolution of intelligence and access to the cognitive unconscious. In J.M Sprague & A.N. Epstein (Eds.), *Progress in psychobiology and physiological psychology, Vol. 6*. New York: Academic Press.

Rozin, P. (1990). Development in the food domain. *Developmental Psychology*, *26*, 555–562.

Rozin, P. & Fallon, A.E. (1987). A perspective on disgust. *Psychological Review*, *94*, 23–41.

Rozin, P., Fallon, A., & Augustoni-Ziskind, M. (1985). The child's conception of food: The development of contamination sensitivity to "disgusting" substances. *Developmental Psychology*, *21*, 1075–1079.

Rozin, P. & Schull, J. (1988). The adaptive-evolutionary point of view in experimental psychology. In R. Atkinson, R.J. Herrnstein, G. Lindzey, & R.D. Luce (Eds.), *Hand-*

book of Experimental Psychology (pp. 503–546). New York: Wiley.

Rubin, K.H. & Mills, R.S.L. (1988). The many faces of social isolation in childhood. *Journal of Consulting and Clinical Psychology, 56,* 916–924.

Ruble, D.N., Balaban, T., & Cooper, J. (1981). Gender constancy and the effects of sex-typed televised toy commercials. *Child Development, 52,* 667–673.

Samuel, J. & Bryant, P. (1984). Asking only one question in the conservation experiment. *Journal of Child Psychology and Psychiatry, 25,* 315–318.

Sanderson, J.A. & Siegal, M. (1988). Conceptions of moral and social rules in rejected and nonrejected preschoolers. *Journal of Clinical Child Psychology, 17,* 66–72.

Schiff, W. (1983). Conservation of length redux: A perceptual-linguistic phenomenon. *Child Development, 54,* 1497–1506.

Selman, R.L. (1980). *The growth of interpersonal understanding: Developmental and clinical analyses.* New York: Academic Press.

Shatz, M. & Gelman, R. (1973). The development of communication skills: Modifications in the speech of young children as a function of listener. *Monographs of the Society for Research in Child Development, 38,* (5, Serial No. 152).

Shatz, M., Wellman, H.H., & Silber, S. (1983). The acquisition of mental verbs: A sytematic investigation of the first reference to mental state. *Cognition, 14,* 301–321.

Shultz, T.R. (1982a). Causal reasoning in the social and nonsocial realms. *Canadian Journal of Behavioral Science, 14,* 307–322.

Shultz, T.R. (1982b). Rules of causal attribution. *Monographs of the Society for Research in Child Development, 1,* Serial No. 194.

Shultz, T.R., Fisher, G.W., Pratt, C.C., & Ruff, S. (1986). Selection of causal rules. *Child Development, 57,* 143–152.

Shultz, T.R., Wright, K., & Schleifer, M. (1986). Assignment of moral responsibility and punishment. *Child Development, 57,* 177–184.

Shweder, R.A. (1977). Likeness and likelihood in everyday thought: Magical thinking in judgments about personality. *Current Anthropology, 18,* 637–658.

Shweder, R.A. (1986). Divergent rationalities. In D.W. Fiske & R.A. Shweder (Eds.), *Metatheory in social science.* Chicago: University of Chicago Press.

Siegal, M. (1982). *Fairness in children.* London: Academic Press.

Siegal, M. (1985). *Children, parenthood, and social welfare.* Oxford: Oxford University Press.

Siegal, M. (1987). Are sons and daughters treated more differently by fathers than by mothers? *Developmental Review, 7,* 183–206.

Siegal, M. (1988a). Children's knowledge of contagion and contamination as causes of illness. *Child Development, 59,* 1353–1359.

Siegal, M. (1988b). Culture, social knowledge, and the determination of criminal responsibility in children: Issues in justice for Aboriginal youth. *Australian Psychologist, 23,* 171–182.

Siegal, M. (1989). *Language and children's representation of number and identity: Are we tapping into a fraction of understanding?* Paper presented at the Conference on Socially Shared Cognition. Learning Research and Development Center, University of Pittsburgh.

Siegal, M. & Barclay, M.S. (1985). Children's evaluations of fathers' socialization behaviors. *Developmental Psychology, 21,* 1090–1096.

Siegal, M. & Cowen, J. (1984). Appraisals of intervention: The mother's versus the culprit's behavior as determinants of children's evaluations of discipline techniques. *Child Development, 55,* 1760–1766.

Siegal, M. & Robinson, J. (1987). Order effects in children's gender constancy responses. *Developmental Psychology, 23,* 283–286.

Siegal, M. & Share, D.L. (1990). Contamination sensitivity in young children. *Developmental Psychology*, *26*, 455–458.

Siegal, M., Share, D.L., & Robinson, J. (1989). Mechanisms of development: Is the real candidate the distinction between appearance and reality? In M.A. Luczcz & T. Nettelbeck (Eds.), *Psychological development: Perspectives across the life-span*. Amsterdam: Elsevier Science.

Siegal, M. & Storey, R.M. (1985). Daycare and children's conceptions of moral and social rules. *Child Development*, *56*, 1001–1008.

Siegal, M., Waters, L.J., & Dinwiddy, L.S. (1988). Misleading children: Causal attributions for inconsistency under repeated questioning. *Journal of Experimental Child Psychology*, *45*, 438–456.

Siegler, R.S. (1981). Developmental sequences within and between concepts. *Monographs of the Society for Research in Child Developmnet*, *46*, Serial No. 189.

Siegler, R.S. (1986). *Children's thinking*. Englewood Cliffs, N.J.: Prentice-Hall.

Sigel, I.E. (1981). Social experience in the development of representational thought: Distancing theory. In I.E. Sigel, D.M. Brodzinsky, & R.M Golinkoff (Eds.), *New Directions in Piagetian theory and practice*. Hillsdale, N.J.: Lawrence Erlbaum Associates Inc.

Slaby, R.G. & Frey, K.S. (1975). Development of gender constancy and selective attention to same-sex models. *Child Development*, *46*, 849–856.

Slade, A. (1987). Quality of attachment and early symbolic play. *Developmental Psychology*, *23*, 78–85.

Smetana, J.G. (1981). Preschool children's conceptions of moral and social rules. *Child Development*, *52*, 1333–1336.

Smetana, J.G. (1985). Preschool children's conceptions of transgressions: The effects of varying moral and conventional domain-related attributes. *Developmental Psychology*, *21*, 18–29.

Smetana, J.G. & Letourneau, K.J. (1984). Development of gender constancy and children's sex-typed free play behavior. *Developmental Psychology*, *20*, 691–696.

Smith, C.L. (1979). Children's understanding of natural language hierarchies. *Journal of Experimental Child Psychology*, *27*, 437–458.

Smith, L. (1985). Making educational sense of Piaget's theory. *Oxford Review of Education*, *11*, 181–191.

Sobol, M.P. & Earn, B.M. (1985). Assessment of children's attributions from social experiences: Implications for social skills training. In B.H. Schneider, K.H. Rubin, & J.E. Ledingham (Eds.), *Childrens' peer relations: Issues in assessment and intervention*. New York: Springer-Verlag.

Sobol, M.P., Earn, B.M., Bennett, D., & Humphries, T. (1983). A categorical analysis of social attributions of learning-disabled children. *Journal of Abnormal Child Psychology*, *11*, 217–228.

Sophian, C. & Huber, A. (1984). Early development in children's causal judgements. *Child Development*, *55*, 512–526.

Spelke, E.S. (1981). The infant's acquisition of bimodally specified events. *Journal of Experimental Child Psychology*, *31*, 279–299.

Sperber, D. & Wilson, D. (1986). *Relevance*. Oxford: Blackwell.

Stanovich, K.E. (1986). Matthew effects in reading: Some consequences of individual differences in the acquisition of literacy. *Reading Research Quarterly*, *21*, 360–406.

Starkey, P. & Cooper, R.G. (1980). Perception of numbers by human infants. *Science*, *210*, 1033–1035.

Starkey, P., Spelke, E.S., & Gelman, R. (1983). Detection of intermodal number correspondences by human infants. *Science*, *222*, 179–181.

Stevenson, H.W., Lee, S.Y., & Stigler, J.W. (1986). Mathematics achievement of Chinese, Japanese, and American children. *Science*, *231*, 693–699.

Sugarman, S. (1987). *Piaget's construction of the child's reality*. New York: Cambridge University Press.

Tauber, M.A. (1979). Sex differences in parent-child interaction styles during a free-play situation. *Child Development*, *50*, 981–988.

Tisak, M.S. (1986). Children's conceptions of parental authority. *Child Development*, *57*, 166–176.

Turiel, E. (1983). *The development of social knowledge: Morality and convention*. New York: Cambridge University Press.

Turiel, E. (1989). Domain-specific social judgment and domain ambiguities. *Merrill-Palmer Quarterly*, *35*, 89–114.

Turiel, E., Nucci, L.P., & Smetana, J.G. (1988). A cross-cultural comparison about what? A critique of Nisan's (1987) study of morality and convention. *Developmental Psychology*, *24*, 140–143.

Ullian, D. (1984). "Why are girls good": A constructivist view. *Sex Roles*, *11*, 241–256.

Uttal, D., Lummis, M., & Stevenson, H. (1988). Low and high mathematics achievement in Japanese, Chinese, and American elementary-school children. *Developmental Psychology*, *24*, 335–342.

Vygotsky, L.S. (1962). *Thought and language*. Cambridge, MA: MIT Press.

Warren, R.M. & Warren, R.P. (1968). *Helmholtz on perception*. New York: Wiley.

Waters, H.S. & Tinsley, V.S. (1985). Evaluating the discriminant and convergent validity of developmental constructs: Another look at egocentrism. *Psychological Bulletin*, *97*, 483–496.

Weinraub, M., Clemens, L.P., Sockloff, A., Ethridge, T., Gracely, E., & Myers, B. (1984). The development of sex role stereotypes in the third year: Relationships to gender labelling, gender identity, sex-types toy preference, and family characteristics. *Child Development*, *55*, 1493–1503.

Wellman, H.M. & Bartsch, K. (1988). Young children's reasoning about beliefs. *Cognition*, *30*, 239–277.

Wellman, H.M. & Estes, D. (1986). Early understanding of mental entities: A reexamination of childhood realism. *Child Development*, *57*, 910–923.

Weston, D. & Turiel, E. (1980). Act-rule relations: Children's concepts of social rules. *Developmental Psychology*, *116*, 417–424.

Wilkening, F. (1981). Integrating velocity, time, and distance information: A developmental study. *Cognitive Psychology*, *13*, 231–247.

Wilkening, F. (1982). Children's knowledge about time, distance, and velocity interrelations. In W.J. Friedman (Ed.), *The developmental psychology of time*. New York: Academic Press.

Wilkening, F., Levin, I., & Druyan, S. (1987). Children's counting strategies for time quantification and integration. *Developmental Psychology*, *23*, 823–831.

Willis, G.B. & Fuson, K.C. (1988). Teaching children to use schematic drawings to solve addition and subtraction word problems. *Journal of Educational Psychology*, *80*, 192–201.

Winer, G., Hemphill, J., & Craig, R.K. (1988). The effect of misleading questions in promoting nonconservation responses in children and adults. *Developmental Psychology*, *24*, 197–202.

Wood, D.J. (1988). *How children think and learn*. Oxford: Basil Blackwell.

Yuill, N. & Perner, J. (1987). Exceptions to mutual trust: Children's use of second-order beliefs in responsibility attribution. *International Journal of Behavioral Development*, *10*, 207–223.

Zigler, E.F. (1987). Formal schooling for four-year-olds? No. *American Psychologist*, *42*, 254–260.

Author Index

Subject Index